MW01273406

Welcome to the "Ninja CREAMi Cookbook for Beginners". As a professional chef with many years of experience in American frozen dessert cuisine, I'm thrilled to share with you the secrets of making incredible frozen treats using the innovative Ninja CREAMi.

Ice cream has long been a beloved staple in American kitchens, a symbol of joy and celebration. From classic vanilla cones enjoyed at summer fairs to gourmet gelatos savored in upscale eateries, the world of frozen desserts offers endless possibilities. However, creating these delights at home often seemed daunting, requiring specialized skills and equipment. That's where the Ninja CREAMi comes in, revolutionizing the way we approach homemade ice cream and beyond.

This cookbook is a treasure trove for anyone eager to dive into the art of making frozen desserts. Whether you're a novice in the kitchen or a seasoned home chef looking to expand your repertoire, you'll find this guide incredibly user-friendly and inspiring. With over 170 recipes, there's something here for every taste and occasion. From rich and creamy ice creams to light and refreshing sorbets, decadent gelatos, creative mix-ins, nutritious smoothie bowls, and indulgent milkshakes, this book covers it all.

The beauty of the Ninja CREAMi lies in its simplicity and versatility. It empowers you to craft delicious, high-quality frozen treats with ease. Each recipe in this book is designed to be straightforward and approachable, ensuring that even beginners can achieve professional results. Additionally, the included nutritional information allows you to enjoy these desserts mindfully, accommodating a range of dietary preferences and needs.

The world of frozen desserts is one of creativity and delight, and with the Ninja CREAMi, the possibilities are truly endless. Imagine serving your family and friends a perfectly churned homemade ice cream, or surprising them with an unexpected flavor combination. With this book as your guide, you can turn these dreams into reality.

So, grab your Ninja CREAMi, and let's get started on this delicious journey together. Here's to many delightful scoops ahead!

Overview of the Ninja Creami Ice Cream Maker

- **Versatility:** The Ninja Creami is not just an ice cream maker; it's a multi-functional kitchen appliance that can also make frozen yogurt, gelato, sorbet, and various other frozen treats. This versatility makes it appealing to users who enjoy experimenting with different dessert recipes.

- **Variety of Settings:** It typically comes with multiple settings and pre-programmed modes for different types of frozen desserts. These settings ensure that you can achieve the desired consistency and texture for your ice cream or other treats.

- **Capacity:** The Ninja Creami usually comes in different sizes, with varying capacities to suit different needs. Whether you're making a small batch for yourself or a larger one for a gathering, there's likely a size that fits your requirements.

- **Ease of Use:** Many users appreciate how easy it is to use the Ninja Creami. It often features intuitive controls and a straightforward process for making ice cream and other frozen treats. Some models may also come with recipe books or online resources to help you get started.

- **Fast Freezing:** One of the key features of the Ninja Creami is its ability to freeze ingredients quickly, allowing you to enjoy your homemade treats in a relatively short amount of time compared to traditional ice cream makers.

- **Cleaning:** Depending on the model, the Ninja Creami may have dishwasher-safe parts, making cleanup a breeze after you've finished making your desserts.

- **Design:** The design of the Ninja Creami is often sleek and modern, fitting well into most kitchen aesthetics. Its compact size also makes it easy to store when not in use.

The Art of Ice Cream Making

◆◆◆

- **Ingredients:** The foundation of any good ice cream is its ingredients. Typically, these include cream, milk, sugar, and flavorings such as vanilla extract or fruit purees. High-quality ingredients can significantly impact the final taste and texture of the ice cream.

- **Balance of Ingredients:** Achieving the perfect balance of ingredients is crucial. The ratio of cream to milk affects the richness and creaminess of the ice cream, while the amount of sugar impacts sweetness and texture. Balancing these elements ensures a harmonious flavor and a smooth, creamy texture.

- **Flavor Development:** Ice cream making allows for endless flavor possibilities. Whether you're using fresh fruits, nuts, chocolates, spices, or other ingredients, the key is to balance flavors and create a well-rounded taste profile. Experimenting with different combinations can lead to unique and delicious creations.

- **Texture:** Texture is a hallmark of great ice cream. Achieving the ideal texture involves careful control of temperature and churning. Properly incorporating air into the mixture through churning creates a light and creamy texture, while preventing the formation of ice crystals ensures a smooth mouthfeel.

- **Churning:** Churning is the process of agitating the ice cream mixture while it freezes, which helps incorporate air and prevent the formation of large ice crystals. The duration and speed of churning can vary depending on the desired consistency and texture of the ice cream.

- **Temperature Control:** Temperature control is critical throughout the ice cream making process. Freezing the mixture at the right temperature ensures proper crystallization and texture development, while allowing the ice cream to temper slightly before serving enhances its scoopability and creaminess.

- **Presentation:** Presentation is the final touch in the art of ice cream making. Whether you're scooping it into cones, bowls, or creating elaborate sundaes, attention to detail can elevate the overall experience. Garnishes, sauces, and toppings add visual appeal and additional layers of flavor and texture.

- **Creativity and Innovation:** The art of ice cream making encourages creativity and innovation. From classic flavors to avant-garde combinations, there's always room for experimentation and pushing the boundaries of traditional techniques to create something truly unique and memorable.

Tips and Tricks for Perfect Ice Cream

- **Use Quality Ingredients:** Start with fresh, high-quality ingredients for the best flavor and texture. Use full-fat dairy for richness and creaminess.

- **Pre-Chill Ingredients:** Before churning, make sure your ice cream base is well chilled. This helps it freeze faster and churn more efficiently.

- **Don't Overheat the Base:** When making the base, heat it gently and avoid boiling. Overheating can result in a grainy texture or curdled appearance.

- **Properly Temper Eggs:** If your recipe calls for eggs, temper them slowly with the hot milk mixture to prevent them from scrambling.

- **Add Flavorings Carefully:** If using flavorings like extracts or alcohol, add them sparingly to avoid overpowering the base. Taste as you go and adjust accordingly.

- **Chill the Churner:** Before churning, chill your ice cream maker's bowl in the freezer overnight. A colder bowl leads to faster freezing and smoother ice cream.

- **Churn Until Just Right:** Pay attention to the consistency of the ice cream as it churns. It should be thick and creamy, with a soft-serve texture. Avoid over-churning, which can result in a grainy or icy texture.

- **Mix-Ins at the Right Time:** If adding mix-ins like nuts or chocolate chips, add them towards the end of churning to evenly distribute them without crushing or sinking.

- **Freeze Properly:** Transfer the churned ice cream to a freezer-safe container and press a piece of plastic wrap directly onto the surface to prevent ice crystals from forming. Seal tightly with a lid and freeze until firm.

- **Aging Improves Flavor:** Allow the ice cream to "age" in the freezer for a few hours or overnight before serving. This allows the flavors to meld and the texture to stabilize.

- **Serve with Style:** For an extra special touch, serve your ice cream in chilled bowls or cones. Garnish with complementary toppings like fresh fruit, chocolate shavings, or a drizzle of caramel sauce.

- **Clean Your Equipment:** Properly clean and dry your ice cream maker after each use to prevent off-flavors and maintain performance.

Table of Content

Ice Cream

Sorbet

Table of Content

Table of Content

Vanilla Bean Ice Cream

 Serves: 8 ; Prep: 20 Min

Ingredient

- 4 egg yolks
- 80g caster sugar
- 300ml double cream
- 300ml whole milk
- 2 vanilla pods, split and seeds scraped out

Instruction:

1. Whisk egg yolks and caster sugar until pale and creamy.
2. Heat double cream, whole milk, and vanilla pods in a saucepan until simmering.
3. Slowly pour hot mixture into egg yolks, whisking constantly.
4. Return mixture to saucepan, cook over low heat until slightly thickened.
5. Strain mixture into a bowl, cool to room temperature, then refrigerate for at least 4 hours.
6. Pour chilled mixture into Ninja CREAMi tub. Freeze for 24 hours.
7. Remove tub, follow assembly and processing instructions in Quick Start Guide.
8. Select ICE CREAM program.
9. Once processing is complete, serve immediately.

Per Serving

Calories: 235; Fat: 19g;
Carbohydrates: 14g; Protein: 4g

CHAPTER 01: ICE CREAM

Chocolate Fudge Ice Cream

 Serves: 8 ; Prep: 20 Min

Ingredient

- 100g dark chocolate, chopped
- 80g caster sugar
- 300ml double cream
- 300ml whole milk
- 20g cocoa powder
- 1 teaspoon vanilla extract

Instruction:

1. In a heatproof bowl, melt the dark chocolate in the microwave in 30-second intervals, stirring until smooth. Set aside to cool slightly.
2. In a separate bowl, whisk together the caster sugar, cocoa powder, and vanilla extract until well combined.
3. In a saucepan, heat the double cream and whole milk over medium heat until just simmering.
4. Slowly pour the hot cream mixture into the sugar mixture, whisking constantly until smooth.
5. Add the melted chocolate to the mixture and whisk until fully incorporated.
6. Pour the mixture into the Ninja CREAMi tub. Place the lid on the tub and freeze for 24 hours.
7. Remove the tub from the freezer and follow the assembly and processing instructions in the Quick Start Guide.
8. Select the ICE CREAM program.
9. Once processing is complete, serve immediately or add additional mix-ins if desired.

Per Serving

Calories: 280; Fat: 20g;
Carbohydrates: 23g; Protein: 3g

Strawberry Ice Cream

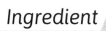 Serves: 8 ; Prep: 15 Min

Ingredient

- 300g fresh strawberries, hulled and chopped
- 80g caster sugar
- 300ml double cream
- 300ml whole milk
- 1 teaspoon vanilla extract

Per Serving

Calories: 180; Fat: 12g;
Carbohydrates: 16g; Protein: 2g

Instruction:

1. In a blender or food processor, blend the fresh strawberries until smooth.
2. In a bowl, combine the blended strawberries with the caster sugar and vanilla extract, stirring until sugar is dissolved.
3. In a saucepan, heat the double cream and whole milk over medium heat until just simmering.
4. Slowly pour the hot cream mixture into the strawberry mixture, stirring constantly until well combined.
5. Pour the mixture into the Ninja CREAMi tub. Place the lid on the tub and freeze for 24 hours.
6. Remove the tub from the freezer and follow the assembly and processing instructions in the Quick Start Guide.
7. Select the ICE CREAM program.
8. Once processing is complete, serve immediately or store in the freezer for later enjoyment.

CHAPTER 01: ICE CREAM

Mint Chocolate Chip Ice Cream

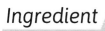 Serves: 8 ; Prep: 10 Min

Ingredient

- 300ml double cream
- 300ml whole milk
- 80g caster sugar
- 1 teaspoon peppermint extract
- Green food coloring (optional)
- 100g dark chocolate, chopped into small chunks

Per Serving

Calories: 240; Fat: 17g;
Carbohydrates: 19g; Protein: 3g

Instruction:

1. In a bowl, mix together the double cream, whole milk, caster sugar, and peppermint extract until sugar is dissolved. Add green food coloring if desired for a minty color.
2. Pour the mixture into the Ninja CREAMi tub. Place the lid on the tub and freeze for 24 hours.
3. Remove the tub from the freezer and follow the assembly and processing instructions in the Quick Start Guide.
4. Select the ICE CREAM program.
5. Once processing is complete, add the chopped dark chocolate chunks into the ice cream and mix gently.
6. Serve immediately or store in the freezer for later enjoyment.

Cookies and Cream Ice Cream

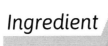 **Serves: 8 ; Prep: 10 Min**

Ingredient

- 300ml double cream
- 300ml whole milk
- 80g caster sugar
- 100g chocolate sandwich cookies, crushed into small pieces

Instruction:

1. In a bowl, mix together the double cream, whole milk, and caster sugar until sugar is dissolved.
2. Pour the mixture into the Ninja CREAMi tub. Place the lid on the tub and freeze for 24 hours.
3. Remove the tub from the freezer and follow the assembly and processing instructions in the Quick Start Guide.
4. Select the ICE CREAM program.
5. Once processing is complete, add the crushed chocolate sandwich cookies into the ice cream and mix gently.
6. Serve immediately or store in the freezer for later enjoyment.

Per Serving

Calories: 230; Fat: 16g;
Carbohydrates: 18g; Protein: 3g

CHAPTER 01: ICE CREAM

Coffee Ice Cream

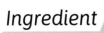 **Serves: 8 ; Prep: 10 Min**

Ingredient

- 300ml double cream
- 300ml whole milk
- 80g caster sugar
- 2 tablespoons instant coffee granules
- 1 teaspoon vanilla extract

Instruction:

1. In a bowl, mix together the double cream, whole milk, caster sugar, instant coffee granules, and vanilla extract until sugar and coffee are dissolved.
2. Pour the mixture into the Ninja CREAMi tub. Place the lid on the tub and freeze for 24 hours.
3. Remove the tub from the freezer and follow the assembly and processing instructions in the Quick Start Guide.
4. Select the ICE CREAM program.
5. Once processing is complete, serve immediately or store in the freezer for later enjoyment.

Per Serving

Calories: 180; Fat: 13g;
Carbohydrates: 14g; Protein: 2g

Peanut Butter Swirl Ice Cream

 **Serves: 8 ; Prep: 15 Min**

Ingredient

- 300ml double cream
- 300ml whole milk
- 80g caster sugar
- 100g peanut butter
- 1 teaspoon vanilla extract

Per Serving

Calories: 250; Fat: 19g;
Carbohydrates: 16g; Protein: 6g

 Instruction:

1. In a saucepan, heat the double cream, whole milk, and caster sugar over medium heat until just simmering, stirring occasionally until sugar is dissolved.
2. Remove from heat and stir in the vanilla extract. Allow the mixture to cool slightly.
3. In a small bowl, microwave the peanut butter for 30 seconds until it becomes pourable.
4. Pour half of the ice cream base into the Ninja CREAMi tub. Drizzle half of the melted peanut butter on top. Repeat with the remaining ice cream base and peanut butter, swirling gently with a spoon or spatula.
5. Place the lid on the tub and freeze for 24 hours.
6. Remove the tub from the freezer and follow the assembly and processing instructions in the Quick Start Guide.
7. Select the ICE CREAM program.
8. Once processing is complete, serve immediately or store in the freezer for later enjoyment.

CHAPTER 01: ICE CREAM

Rocky Road Ice Cream

  Serves: 8 ; Prep: 20 Min

Ingredient

- 300ml double cream
- 300ml whole milk
- 80g caster sugar
- 50g dark chocolate, chopped
- 50g milk chocolate, chopped
- 50g mini marshmallows
- 50g chopped almonds

Per Serving

Calories: 280; Fat: 20g;
Carbohydrates: 21g; Protein: 4g

Instruction:

1. In a saucepan, heat the double cream, whole milk, and caster sugar over medium heat until just simmering, stirring occasionally until sugar is dissolved.
2. Remove from heat and allow the mixture to cool slightly.
3. Pour the mixture into the Ninja CREAMi tub. Place the lid on the tub and freeze for 24 hours.
4. Remove the tub from the freezer and follow the assembly and processing instructions in the Quick Start Guide.
5. Select the ICE CREAM program.
6. Once processing is complete, add the chopped dark chocolate, milk chocolate, mini marshmallows, and chopped almonds into the ice cream and mix gently.
7. Serve immediately or store in the freezer for later enjoyment.

Pistachio Ice Cream

  ## Instruction:

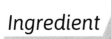 **Serves: 8 ; Prep: 15 Min**

Ingredient

- 300ml double cream
- 300ml whole milk
- 80g caster sugar
- 100g shelled pistachios, finely chopped
- 1 teaspoon almond extract
- Green food coloring (optional)

1. In a bowl, mix together the double cream, whole milk, caster sugar, and almond extract until sugar is dissolved.
2. Add the finely chopped pistachios to the mixture and stir until evenly distributed. Add green food coloring if desired for a vibrant color.
3. Pour the mixture into the Ninja CREAMi tub. Place the lid on the tub and freeze for 24 hours.
4. Remove the tub from the freezer and follow the assembly and processing instructions in the Quick Start Guide.
5. Select the ICE CREAM program.
6. Once processing is complete, serve immediately or store in the freezer for later enjoyment.

Per Serving

Calories: 250; Fat: 19g;
Carbohydrates: 16g; Protein: 3g

CHAPTER 01: ICE CREAM

Salted Caramel Ice Cream

  ## Instruction:

 Serves: 8 ; Prep: 15 Min

Ingredient

- 300ml double cream
- 300ml whole milk
- 80g caster sugar
- 100g soft caramel candies
- 1/2 teaspoon sea salt flakes

1. In a saucepan, heat the double cream, whole milk, and caster sugar over medium heat until just simmering, stirring occasionally until sugar is dissolved.
2. Remove from heat and stir in the sea salt flakes until dissolved.
3. Allow the mixture to cool slightly, then pour it into the Ninja CREAMi tub.
4. Place the soft caramel candies in a microwave-safe bowl and heat in the microwave for 30 seconds or until melted.
5. Drizzle the melted caramel over the ice cream mixture in the tub.
6. Place the lid on the tub and freeze for 24 hours.
7. Remove the tub from the freezer and follow the assembly and processing instructions in the Quick Start Guide.
8. Select the ICE CREAM program.
9. Once processing is complete, serve immediately or store in the freezer for later enjoyment.

Per Serving

Calories: 230; Fat: 16g;
Carbohydrates: 20g; Protein: 2g

Coconut Ice Cream

Serves: 8   ; Prep: 05 Min

Ingredient

- 300ml coconut cream
- 300ml whole milk
- 80g caster sugar
- 1 teaspoon vanilla extract
- Shredded coconut for garnish (optional)

 **Instruction:**

1. In a bowl, whisk together the coconut cream, whole milk, caster sugar, and vanilla extract until sugar is dissolved.
2. Pour the mixture into the Ninja CREAMi tub. Place the lid on the tub and freeze for 24 hours.
3. Remove the tub from the freezer and follow the assembly and processing instructions in the Quick Start Guide.
4. Select the ICE CREAM program.
5. Once processing is complete, serve immediately, garnished with shredded coconut if desired, or store in the freezer for later enjoyment.

Per Serving

Calories: 220; Fat: 17g;
Carbohydrates: 16g; Protein: 2g

CHAPTER 01: ICE CREAM

Banana Nut Ice Cream

Serves: 8   ; Prep: 10 Min

Ingredient

- 3 ripe bananas, peeled and sliced
- 300ml double cream
- 300ml whole milk
- 80g caster sugar
- 50g chopped walnuts

Instruction:

1. In a blender, combine the sliced bananas, double cream, whole milk, and caster sugar. Blend until smooth.
2. Pour the mixture into the Ninja CREAMi tub. Place the lid on the tub and freeze for 24 hours.
3. Remove the tub from the freezer and follow the assembly and processing instructions in the Quick Start Guide.
4. Select the ICE CREAM program.
5. Once processing is complete, add the chopped walnuts into the ice cream and mix gently.
6. Serve immediately or store in the freezer for later enjoyment.

Per Serving

Calories: 220; Fat: 15g;
Carbohydrates: 20g; Protein: 3g

Blackberry Ice Cream

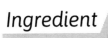 **Serves: 8 ; Prep: 10 Min**

Ingredient

- 300g fresh blackberries
- 300ml double cream
- 300ml whole milk
- 80g caster sugar
- 1 teaspoon vanilla extract

Per Serving

Calories: 220; Fat: 15g;
Carbohydrates: 20g; Protein: 2g

 ## Instruction:

1. In a blender, puree the fresh blackberries until smooth.
2. In a mixing bowl, combine the blackberry puree, double cream, whole milk, caster sugar, and vanilla extract. Mix until well combined.
3. Pour the mixture into the Ninja CREAMi tub. Place the lid on the tub and freeze for 24 hours.
4. Remove the tub from the freezer and follow the assembly and processing instructions in the Quick Start Guide.
5. Select the ICE CREAM program.
6. Once processing is complete, serve immediately or store in the freezer for later enjoyment.

Raspberry Swirl Ice Cream

 **Serves: 8 ; Prep: 15 Min**

Ingredient

- 300g fresh raspberries
- 300ml double cream
- 300ml whole milk
- 80g caster sugar
- 1 teaspoon vanilla extract

Raspberry Swirl:
- 100g fresh raspberries
- 2 tablespoons caster sugar

Per Serving

Calories: 210; Fat: 14g;
Carbohydrates: 20g; Protein: 2g

 ## Instruction:

1. In a blender, puree the fresh raspberries until smooth. Strain through a fine mesh sieve to remove seeds, if desired.
2. In a mixing bowl, combine the strained raspberry puree, double cream, whole milk, caster sugar, and vanilla extract. Mix until well combined.
3. Pour the mixture into the Ninja CREAMi tub. Place the lid on the tub and freeze for 24 hours.
4. In a small saucepan, combine the remaining fresh raspberries and caster sugar. Cook over medium heat until the raspberries break down and the mixture thickens slightly, about 5-7 minutes. Remove from heat and let it cool.
5. Once the ice cream base has chilled, remove the tub from the freezer and follow the assembly and processing instructions in the Quick Start Guide.
6. Select the ICE CREAM program.
7. Once processing is complete, drizzle the raspberry swirl over the churned ice cream and gently fold it in using a spatula, creating swirls.
8. Serve immediately for soft-serve consistency, or transfer the ice cream to a freezer-safe container and freeze for firmer ice cream.

Mango Ice Cream

Serves: 8 ; Prep: 10 Min

Ingredient

- 400g ripe mangoes, peeled and diced
- 300ml double cream
- 300ml whole milk
- 80g caster sugar
- 1 teaspoon vanilla extract

 Instruction:

1. In a blender, puree the diced mangoes until smooth.
2. In a mixing bowl, combine the mango puree, double cream, whole milk, caster sugar, and vanilla extract. Mix until well combined.
3. Pour the mixture into the Ninja CREAMi tub. Place the lid on the tub and freeze for 24 hours.
4. Once the ice cream base has chilled, remove the tub from the freezer and follow the assembly and processing instructions in the Quick Start Guide.
5. Select the ICE CREAM program.
6. Once processing is complete, remove the tub from the Ninja CREAMi. Use a spatula to transfer the ice cream to a freezer-safe container.
7. Place the lid on the container and freeze for an additional 2-3 hours, or until firm.
8. Serve and enjoy!

Per Serving

Calories: 180; Fat: 11g;
Carbohydrates: 18g; Protein: 2g

CHAPTER 01: ICE CREAM

Pineapple Coconut Ice Cream

Serves: 6 ; Prep: 10 Min

Ingredient

- 400g pineapple chunks, fresh or canned
- 200ml coconut milk
- 200ml double cream
- 50g caster sugar
- 1 teaspoon vanilla extract

Instruction:

1. In a blender, puree the pineapple chunks until smooth.
2. In a mixing bowl, combine the pineapple puree, coconut milk, double cream, caster sugar, and vanilla extract. Mix until well combined.
3. Pour the mixture into the Ninja CREAMi tub. Place the lid on the tub and freeze for 24 hours.
4. Once the ice cream base has chilled, remove the tub from the freezer and follow the assembly and processing instructions in the Quick Start Guide.
5. Select the ICE CREAM program.
6. Once processing is complete, remove the tub from the Ninja CREAMi. Use a spatula to transfer the ice cream to a freezer-safe container.
7. Place the lid on the container and freeze for an additional 2-3 hours, or until firm.
8. Serve and enjoy!

Per Serving

Calories: 210; Fat: 15g;
Carbohydrates: 20g; Protein: 2g

Lemon Sorbet Ice Cream

 **Serves: 6 ; Prep: 10 Min**

Ingredient

- 200ml lemon juice (from about 4-6 lemons)
- 200g caster sugar
- 400ml water
- Zest of 1 lemon

Per Serving

Calories: 140; Fat: 0g;
Carbohydrates: 36g; Protein: 0g

Instruction:

1. In a saucepan, combine the caster sugar and water. Heat over medium heat, stirring constantly, until the sugar is completely dissolved. Remove from heat and let it cool.
2. Once the sugar syrup has cooled, add the lemon juice and lemon zest. Stir until well combined.
3. Pour the mixture into the Ninja CREAMi tub. Place the lid on the tub and freeze for 24 hours.
4. After 24 hours, remove the tub from the freezer and follow the assembly and processing instructions in the Quick Start Guide.
5. Select the ICE CREAM program.
6. Once processing is complete, remove the tub from the Ninja CREAMi. Use a spatula to transfer the sorbet to a freezer-safe container.
7. Place the lid on the container and freeze for an additional 2-3 hours, or until firm.
8. Serve and enjoy!

Blueberry Cheesecake Ice Cream

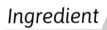 **Serves: 6 ; Prep: 15 Min**

Ingredient

- 200g cream cheese, softened
- 100g caster sugar
- 150ml double cream
- 230ml whole milk
- 100g fresh blueberries
- 50g digestive biscuits, crushed

Per Serving

Calories: 280; Fat: 20g;
Carbohydrates: 21g; Protein: 4g

Instruction:

1. In a large bowl, beat together the softened cream cheese and caster sugar until smooth and creamy.
2. Slowly mix in the double cream and whole milk until fully combined.
3. Add the fresh blueberries and crushed digestive biscuits to the mixture and gently fold them in.
4. Pour the base into an empty tub. Place the lid on the tub and freeze for 24 hours.
5. After 24 hours, remove the tub from the freezer and follow the assembly and processing instructions in the Quick Start Guide.
6. Select the ICE CREAM program.
7. Once processing is complete, remove the tub from the Ninja CREAMi. Serve immediately or transfer to a freezer-safe container and freeze for an additional 1-2 hours for a firmer texture.
8. Enjoy your delicious blueberry cheesecake ice cream!

Chocolate Peanut Butter Cup Ice Cream

Serves: 6 ; Prep: 20 Min

Ingredient

- 150g dark chocolate, chopped
- 50g smooth peanut butter
- 100g caster sugar
- 150ml double cream
- 230ml whole milk
- 50g peanut butter cups, chopped

Per Serving

Calories: 300; Fat: 20g;
Carbohydrates: 25g; Protein: 5g

Instruction:

1. In a microwave-safe bowl, melt the dark chocolate and smooth peanut butter together in short intervals until smooth.
2. In a separate large bowl, whisk together the caster sugar, double cream, and whole milk until well combined.
3. Pour the melted chocolate and peanut butter mixture into the bowl with the cream and milk mixture. Stir until fully combined.
4. Pour the base into an empty tub. Place the lid on the tub and freeze for 24 hours.
5. After 24 hours, remove the tub from the freezer and follow the assembly and processing instructions in the Quick Start Guide.
6. Select the ICE CREAM program.
7. Once processing is complete, add the chopped peanut butter cups to the ice cream and stir gently to distribute.
8. Serve immediately for a soft-serve consistency or transfer to a freezer-safe container and freeze for an additional 1-2 hours for a firmer texture.
9. Enjoy your indulgent chocolate peanut butter cup ice cream!

Almond Joy Ice Cream

Serves: 6 ; Prep: 20 Min

Ingredient

- 150g dark chocolate, chopped
- 50g sweetened shredded coconut
- 50g almonds, chopped
- 100g caster sugar
- 150ml double cream
- 230ml whole milk

Per Serving

Calories: 300; Fat: 20g;
Carbohydrates: 25g; Protein: 5g

Instruction:

1. In a microwave-safe bowl, melt the dark chocolate until smooth.
2. In a separate bowl, combine the shredded coconut and chopped almonds.
3. In a large bowl, whisk together the caster sugar, double cream, and whole milk until well combined.
4. Pour the melted chocolate into the cream mixture and stir until fully combined.
5. Add the shredded coconut and chopped almonds to the mixture and stir until evenly distributed.
6. Pour the base into an empty tub. Place the lid on the tub and freeze for 24 hours.
7. After 24 hours, remove the tub from the freezer and follow the assembly and processing instructions in the Quick Start Guide.
8. Select the ICE CREAM program.
9. Once processing is complete, serve immediately for a soft-serve consistency or transfer to a freezer-safe container and freeze for an additional 1-2 hours for a firmer texture.
10. Enjoy your delicious homemade Almond Joy ice cream!

Cherry Garcia Ice Cream

 **Serves: 6 ; Prep: 15 Min**

Ingredient

- 200g cherries, pitted and halved
- 50g dark chocolate, chopped
- 100g caster sugar
- 150ml double cream
- 230ml whole milk

Per Serving

Calories: 180; Fat: 10g;
Carbohydrates: 20g; Protein: 2g

 ## Instruction:

1. In a saucepan, heat the cherries and caster sugar over medium heat until the cherries release their juices and the sugar is dissolved. Remove from heat and let cool completely.
2. In a large bowl, whisk together the double cream and whole milk until well combined.
3. Add the cooled cherry mixture to the cream mixture and stir until evenly distributed.
4. Pour the base into an empty tub. Place the lid on the tub and freeze for 24 hours.
5. After 24 hours, remove the tub from the freezer and follow the assembly and processing instructions in the Quick Start Guide.
6. Select the ICE CREAM program.
7. Once processing is complete, add the chopped dark chocolate to the ice cream and stir to distribute evenly.
8. Serve immediately for a soft-serve consistency or transfer to a freezer-safe container and freeze for an additional 1-2 hours for a firmer texture.
9. Enjoy your delicious homemade Cherry Garcia ice cream!

CHAPTER 01: ICE CREAM

Maple Walnut Ice Cream

 **Serves: 6 ; Prep: 10 Min**

Ingredient

- 100ml maple syrup
- 50g walnuts, chopped
- 50g caster sugar
- 150ml double cream
- 230ml whole milk

Per Serving

Calories: 200; Fat: 12g;
Carbohydrates: 20g; Protein: 3g

 ## Instruction:

1. In a saucepan, heat the maple syrup and caster sugar over low heat until the sugar is dissolved. Let it cool completely.
2. In a large bowl, whisk together the double cream and whole milk until well combined.
3. Add the cooled maple syrup mixture to the cream mixture and stir until evenly distributed.
4. Pour the base into an empty tub. Place the lid on the tub and freeze for 24 hours.
5. After 24 hours, remove the tub from the freezer and follow the assembly and processing instructions in the Quick Start Guide.
6. Select the ICE CREAM program.
7. Once processing is complete, add the chopped walnuts to the ice cream and stir to distribute evenly.
8. Serve immediately for a soft-serve consistency or transfer to a freezer-safe container and freeze for an additional 1-2 hours for a firmer texture.
9. Enjoy your delightful homemade Maple Walnut ice cream!

Orange Creamsicle Ice Cream

Serves: 6 ; Prep: 10 Min

Ingredient

- Zest of 1 orange
- 150g caster sugar
- 250ml double cream
- 250ml whole milk
- 1 teaspoon vanilla extract
- 120ml orange juice (freshly squeezed if possible)

Per Serving

Calories: 250; Fat: 15g;
Carbohydrates: 25g; Protein: 2g

Instruction:

1. In a large bowl, combine the orange zest and caster sugar. Rub the zest into the sugar with your fingers until fragrant.
2. Add the double cream, whole milk, vanilla extract, and orange juice to the bowl. Stir until the sugar is dissolved and everything is well combined.
3. Pour the mixture into the Ninja CREAMi tub.
4. Place the lid on the tub and freeze for 24 hours.
5. After 24 hours, remove the tub from the freezer and follow the assembly and processing instructions in the Quick Start Guide.
6. Select the ICE CREAM program.
7. Once processing is complete, remove the ice cream from the tub and serve immediately for a soft-serve consistency.
8. Enjoy the refreshing taste of homemade Orange Creamsicle ice cream!

CHAPTER 01: ICE CREAM

Key Lime Pie Ice Cream

Serves: 6 ; Prep: 10 Min

Ingredient

- Zest of 2 limes
- 120g caster sugar
- 150ml double cream
- 250ml whole milk
- 1 teaspoon vanilla extract
- 4 tablespoons key lime juice
- 100g graham crackers, crushed
- Additional lime zest for garnish (optional)

Per Serving

Calories: 230; Fat: 12g;
Carbohydrates: 28g; Protein: 3g

Instruction:

1. In a large bowl, combine the lime zest and caster sugar. Rub the zest into the sugar with your fingers until fragrant.
2. Add the double cream, whole milk, vanilla extract, and key lime juice to the bowl. Stir until the sugar is dissolved and everything is well combined.
3. Pour the mixture into the Ninja CREAMi tub.
4. Add the crushed graham crackers to the mixture and gently stir to distribute them evenly.
5. Place the lid on the tub and freeze for 24 hours.
6. After 24 hours, remove the tub from the freezer and follow the assembly and processing instructions in the Quick Start Guide.
7. Select the ICE CREAM program.
8. Once processing is complete, remove the ice cream from the tub and serve immediately for a soft-serve consistency.
9. Garnish with additional lime zest if desired.
10. Enjoy the delightful taste of homemade Key Lime Pie ice cream!

Brownie Batter Ice Cream

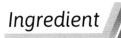 Serves: 4 ; Prep: 05 Min

Ingredient

- 150g brownie mix
- 200ml double cream
- 200ml whole milk
- 60g caster sugar
- 1 teaspoon vanilla extract

Instruction:

1. In a large mixing bowl, combine the brownie mix, double cream, whole milk, caster sugar, and vanilla extract. Stir until the brownie mix is fully incorporated into the mixture.
2. Pour the base into the Ninja CREAMi tub.
3. Place the lid on the tub and freeze for 24 hours.
4. After 24 hours, remove the tub from the freezer and follow the assembly and processing instructions in the Quick Start Guide.
5. Select the ICE CREAM program.
6. Once processing is complete, the brownie batter ice cream is ready to serve.

Per Serving

Calories: 290; Fat: 18g;
Carbohydrates: 29g; Protein: 4g

CHAPTER 01: ICE CREAM

Red Velvet Ice Cream

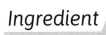 Serves: 4 ; Prep: 05 Min

Ingredient

- 100g red velvet cake mix
- 300ml double cream
- 200ml whole milk
- 60g caster sugar
- 1 teaspoon vanilla extract

Instruction:

1. In a large mixing bowl, combine the red velvet cake mix, double cream, whole milk, caster sugar, and vanilla extract. Stir until the cake mix is fully incorporated into the mixture.
2. Pour the base into the Ninja CREAMi tub.
3. Place the lid on the tub and freeze for 24 hours.
4. After 24 hours, remove the tub from the freezer and follow the assembly and processing instructions in the Quick Start Guide.
5. Select the ICE CREAM program.
6. Once processing is complete, the red velvet ice cream is ready to serve.

Per Serving

Calories: 280; Fat: 18g;
Carbohydrates: 28g; Protein: 3g

Cinnamon Roll Ice Cream

Serves: 4 ; Prep: 10 Min

 Ingredient

- 150ml double cream
- 230ml whole milk
- 50g caster sugar
- 1 teaspoon ground cinnamon
- 1 teaspoon vanilla extract
- 50g crushed cinnamon roll pieces

Instruction:

1. In a mixing bowl, combine double cream, whole milk, caster sugar, ground cinnamon, and vanilla extract. Stir until sugar is dissolved.
2. Pour the mixture into the Ninja CREAMi tub.
3. Add crushed cinnamon roll pieces into the mixture.
4. Pour the base into an empty tub. Place the lid on the tub and freeze for 24 hours.
5. Remove the tub from the freezer, assemble, and select the ICE CREAM program.
6. Once processing is complete, Cinnamon Roll Ice Cream is ready to enjoy.

Per Serving

Calories: 180; Fat: 12g;
Carbohydrates: 16g; Protein: 2g

CHAPTER 01: ICE CREAM

S'mores Ice Cream

 **Serves: 4 ; Prep: 10 Min**

Ingredient

- 150ml double cream
- 230ml whole milk
- 50g caster sugar
- 50g chocolate chips
- 50g mini marshmallows
- 2 digestive biscuits, crushed

Instruction:

1. In a mixing bowl, combine double cream, whole milk, and caster sugar. Stir until sugar is dissolved.
2. Pour the mixture into the Ninja CREAMi tub.
3. Add chocolate chips, mini marshmallows, and crushed digestive biscuits into the mixture.
4. Pour the base into an empty tub. Place the lid on the tub and freeze for 24 hours.
5. Remove the tub from the freezer, assemble, and select the ICE CREAM program.
6. Once processing is complete, S'mores Ice Cream is ready to enjoy.

Per Serving

Calories: 250; Fat: 16g;
Carbohydrates: 24g; Protein: 3g

Tiramisu Ice Cream

 Serves: 4 ; Prep: 10 Min

Ingredient

- 150ml double cream
- 230ml whole milk
- 50g caster sugar
- 1 tablespoon instant coffee powder
- 1 tablespoon coffee liqueur (optional)
- 2 tablespoons cocoa powder
- 50g ladyfinger biscuits, crushed

Instruction:

1. In a mixing bowl, combine double cream, whole milk, caster sugar, instant coffee powder, and coffee liqueur (if using). Stir until the sugar and coffee powder are dissolved.
2. Pour the mixture into the Ninja CREAMi tub.
3. Add cocoa powder and crushed ladyfinger biscuits into the mixture.
4. Pour the base into an empty tub. Place the lid on the tub and freeze for 24 hours.
5. Remove the tub from the freezer, assemble, and select the ICE CREAM program.
6. Once processing is complete, Tiramisu Ice Cream is ready to enjoy.

Per Serving

Calories: 180; Fat: 11g;
Carbohydrates: 18g; Protein: 2g

CHAPTER 01: ICE CREAM

Honey Lavender Ice Cream

 Serves: 4 ; Prep: 10 Min

Ingredient

- 150ml double cream
- 230ml whole milk
- 70g caster sugar
- 2 tablespoons honey
- 1 tablespoon dried culinary lavender

Instruction:

1. In a saucepan, combine the double cream, whole milk, caster sugar, honey, and dried lavender.
2. Heat the mixture over medium heat until it almost reaches a simmer. Do not let it boil.
3. Once heated, remove the saucepan from the heat and let the mixture steep for 15-20 minutes to infuse the lavender flavor.
4. Strain the mixture to remove the dried lavender.
5. Pour the base into an empty tub. Place the lid on the tub and freeze for 24 hours.
6. After freezing, remove the tub from the freezer, assemble, and select the ICE CREAM program.
7. Once processing is complete, Honey Lavender Ice Cream is ready to serve.

Per Serving

Calories: 200; Fat: 12g;
Carbohydrates: 21g; Protein: 2g

White Chocolate Raspberry Ice Cream

Serves: 8 ; Prep: 20 Min

Ingredient

- 150ml double cream
- 230ml whole milk
- 100g white chocolate, chopped
- 50g caster sugar
- 1 teaspoon vanilla extract
- 100g fresh raspberries

Instruction:

1. In a saucepan, heat the double cream and whole milk over medium heat until it begins to simmer.
2. Remove from heat and stir in the chopped white chocolate until melted and smooth.
3. Add the caster sugar and vanilla extract, stirring until the sugar is dissolved.
4. Let the mixture cool to room temperature.
5. Pour the mixture into an empty tub. Drop in the fresh raspberries.
6. Place the lid on the tub and freeze for 24 hours.
7. After freezing, remove the tub from the freezer, assemble, and select the ICE CREAM program.
8. Once processing is complete, White Chocolate Raspberry Ice Cream is ready to serve.

Per Serving

Calories: 250; Fat: 17g;
Carbohydrates: 21g; Protein: 3g

CHAPTER 01: ICE CREAM

Grapefruit Ice Cream

Serves: 4 ; Prep: 10 Min

Ingredient

- 150ml double cream
- 230ml whole milk
- 100g caster sugar
- Zest of 1 grapefruit
- 100ml fresh grapefruit juice

Instruction:

1. In a mixing bowl, combine the double cream, whole milk, caster sugar, and grapefruit zest. Stir until the sugar is dissolved.
2. Stir in the fresh grapefruit juice until well combined.
3. Pour the mixture into an empty tub.
4. Place the lid on the tub and freeze for 24 hours.
5. After freezing, remove the tub from the freezer, assemble, and select the ICE CREAM program.
6. Once processing is complete, Grapefruit Ice Cream is ready to serve.

Per Serving

Calories: 180; Fat: 11g;
Carbohydrates: 19g; Protein: 2g

Lemon Sorbet

Serves: 6   ; Prep: 15 Min

Ingredient

- 250ml water
- 150g granulated sugar
- Zest of 2 lemons
- Juice of 4 lemons

 Instruction:

1. In a saucepan, combine water, granulated sugar, and lemon zest. Heat over medium heat, stirring occasionally, until the sugar is completely dissolved.
2. Remove the saucepan from heat and let the mixture cool to room temperature.
3. Once cooled, stir in the fresh lemon juice.
4. Pour the mixture into an empty tub.
5. Place the lid on the tub and freeze for 24 hours.
6. After freezing, remove the tub from the freezer, assemble, and select the SORBET program.
7. Once processing is complete, Lemon Sorbet is ready to serve.

Per Serving

Calories: 120; Fat: 0g;
Carbohydrates: 32g; Protein: 0g

CHAPTER 02: SORBET

Raspberry Sorbet

Serves: 6   ; Prep: 20 Min

Ingredient

- 250g fresh raspberries
- 150g granulated sugar
- 250ml water
- Juice of 1 lemon

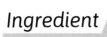 Instruction:

1. In a saucepan, combine water and granulated sugar. Heat over medium heat, stirring occasionally, until the sugar is completely dissolved.
2. Add fresh raspberries to the saucepan and continue to cook until the raspberries break down and the mixture thickens slightly.
3. Remove the saucepan from heat and let the mixture cool to room temperature.
4. Once cooled, blend the raspberry mixture until smooth.
5. Strain the raspberry mixture through a fine mesh sieve to remove seeds.
6. Stir in the lemon juice.
7. Pour the mixture into an empty tub.
8. Place the lid on the tub and freeze for 24 hours.
9. After freezing, remove the tub from the freezer, assemble, and select the SORBET program.
10. Once processing is complete, Raspberry Sorbet is ready to serve.

Per Serving

Calories: 110; Fat: 0g;
Carbohydrates: 28g; Protein: 1g

Mango Sorbet

**Serves: 6   ; Prep: 15 Min**

Ingredient

- 500g ripe mangoes, peeled and diced
- 100g granulated sugar
- Juice of 2 limes
- 250ml water

 Instruction:

1. In a saucepan, combine water and granulated sugar. Heat over medium heat, stirring occasionally, until the sugar is completely dissolved.
2. Add diced mangoes to the saucepan and continue to cook until the mangoes are softened, about 5 minutes.
3. Remove the saucepan from heat and let the mixture cool to room temperature.
4. Once cooled, transfer the mango mixture to a blender.
5. Add the lime juice to the blender and blend until smooth.
6. Pour the mango mixture through a fine mesh sieve to remove any fibrous bits.
7. Pour the strained mixture into an empty tub.
8. Place the lid on the tub and freeze for 24 hours.
9. After freezing, remove the tub from the freezer, assemble, and select the SORBET program.
10. Once processing is complete, Mango Sorbet is ready to serve.

Per Serving

Calories: 130; Fat: 0g;
Carbohydrates: 34g; Protein: 1g

CHAPTER 02: SORBET

Strawberry Sorbet

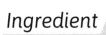**Serves: 6   ; Prep: 15 Min**

Ingredient

- 500g fresh strawberries, hulled
- 100g granulated sugar
- Juice of 1 lemon
- 250ml water

 Instruction:

1. In a saucepan, combine water and granulated sugar. Heat over medium heat, stirring occasionally, until the sugar is completely dissolved.
2. Add hulled strawberries to the saucepan and continue to cook until the strawberries are softened, about 5 minutes.
3. Remove the saucepan from heat and let the mixture cool to room temperature.
4. Once cooled, transfer the strawberry mixture to a blender.
5. Add the lemon juice to the blender and blend until smooth.
6. Pour the strawberry mixture through a fine mesh sieve to remove any seeds.
7. Pour the strained mixture into an empty tub.
8. Place the lid on the tub and freeze for 24 hours.
9. After freezing, remove the tub from the freezer, assemble, and select the SORBET program.
10. Once processing is complete, Strawberry Sorbet is ready to serve.

Per Serving

Calories: 80; Fat: 0g;
Carbohydrates: 20g; Protein: 1g

Pineapple Sorbet

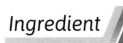 Serves: 6 ; Prep: 15 Min

Ingredient

- 500g pineapple chunks (fresh or frozen)
- 100g granulated sugar
- 250ml water
- Juice of 1 lime

Instruction:

1. In a saucepan, combine water and granulated sugar. Heat over medium heat, stirring occasionally, until the sugar is completely dissolved.
2. Add pineapple chunks to the saucepan and continue to cook until the pineapple is softened, about 5 minutes.
3. Remove the saucepan from heat and let the mixture cool to room temperature.
4. Once cooled, transfer the pineapple mixture to a blender.
5. Add the lime juice to the blender and blend until smooth.
6. Pour the pineapple mixture through a fine mesh sieve to remove any fibers.
7. Pour the strained mixture into an empty tub.
8. Place the lid on the tub and freeze for 24 hours.
9. After freezing, remove the tub from the freezer, assemble, and select the SORBET program.
10. Once processing is complete, Pineapple Sorbet is ready to serve.

Per Serving

Calories: 100; Fat: 0g;
Carbohydrates: 26g; Protein: 1g

CHAPTER 02: SORBET

Watermelon Sorbet

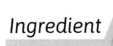 Serves: 6 ; Prep: 10 Min

Ingredient

- 500g watermelon, seeded and cubed
- 100g granulated sugar
- 1 tablespoon fresh lime juice

Instruction:

1. In a blender, combine the watermelon cubes, granulated sugar, and lime juice.
2. Blend until smooth.
3. Pour the mixture through a fine mesh sieve to remove any pulp or seeds.
4. Pour the strained mixture into an empty tub.
5. Place the lid on the tub and freeze for 24 hours.
6. After freezing, remove the tub from the freezer, assemble, and select the SORBET program.
7. Once processing is complete, Watermelon Sorbet is ready to serve.

Per Serving

Calories: 90; Fat: 0g;
Carbohydrates: 23g; Protein: 0.5g

Peach Sorbet

Serves: 6   ; Prep: 10 Min

Ingredient

- 500g ripe peaches, peeled, pitted, and chopped
- 100g granulated sugar
- 1 tablespoon lemon juice

 **Instruction:**

1. In a blender, combine the chopped peaches, granulated sugar, and lemon juice.
2. Blend until smooth.
3. Pour the mixture through a fine mesh sieve to remove any pulp.
4. Pour the strained mixture into an empty tub.
5. Place the lid on the tub and freeze for 24 hours.
6. After freezing, remove the tub from the freezer, assemble, and select the SORBET program.
7. Once processing is complete, Peach Sorbet is ready to serve.

Per Serving

Calories: 100; Fat: 0g;
Carbohydrates: 26g; Protein: 1g

CHAPTER 02: SORBET

Blueberry Sorbet

Serves: 6   ; Prep: 10 Min

Ingredient

- 400g fresh blueberries
- 100g granulated sugar
- 2 tablespoons lemon juice

Instruction:

1. Rinse the blueberries and remove any stems.
2. In a blender, combine the blueberries, granulated sugar, and lemon juice.
3. Blend until smooth.
4. Pour the mixture through a fine mesh sieve to remove any pulp.
5. Pour the strained mixture into an empty tub.
6. Place the lid on the tub and freeze for 24 hours.
7. After freezing, remove the tub from the freezer, assemble, and select the SORBET program.
8. Once processing is complete, Blueberry Sorbet is ready to serve.

Per Serving

Calories: 90; Fat: 0g;
Carbohydrates: 23g; Protein: 1g

Lime Sorbet

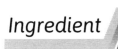 **Serves: 6 ; Prep: 15 Min**

Ingredient

- 250ml freshly squeezed lime juice
- 200g granulated sugar
- 500ml water

Instruction:

1. In a saucepan, combine the granulated sugar and water. Heat over medium heat, stirring occasionally, until the sugar is completely dissolved to make a simple syrup.
2. Remove the syrup from heat and let it cool to room temperature.
3. Once cooled, stir in the freshly squeezed lime juice.
4. Pour the mixture into an empty tub.
5. Place the lid on the tub and freeze for 24 hours.
6. After freezing, remove the tub from the freezer, assemble, and select the SORBET program.
7. Once processing is complete, Lime Sorbet is ready to serve.

__Per Serving__

Calories: 140; Fat: 0g;
Carbohydrates: 36g; Protein: 0g

CHAPTER 02: SORBET

Blackberry Sorbet

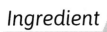 **Serves: 6 ; Prep: 20 Min**

Ingredient

- 400g fresh blackberries
- 150g granulated sugar
- 250ml water
- Juice of 1 lemon

Instruction:

1. In a saucepan, combine the granulated sugar and water. Heat over medium heat, stirring occasionally, until the sugar is completely dissolved to make a simple syrup.
2. Remove the syrup from heat and let it cool to room temperature.
3. In a blender, blend the fresh blackberries until smooth.
4. Strain the blackberry puree through a fine mesh sieve to remove the seeds.
5. Stir the blackberry puree into the cooled simple syrup.
6. Add the lemon juice and mix well.
7. Pour the mixture into an empty tub.
8. Place the lid on the tub and freeze for 24 hours.
9. After freezing, remove the tub from the freezer, assemble, and select the SORBET program.
10. Once processing is complete, Blackberry Sorbet is ready to serve.

__Per Serving__

Calories: 120; Fat: 0g;
Carbohydrates: 30g; Protein: 1g

Orange Sorbet

Serves: 6 ; Prep: 20 Min

Ingredient

- 400ml freshly squeezed orange juice
- Zest of 1 orange
- 150g granulated sugar
- 250ml water
- Juice of 1 lemon

 **Instruction:**

1. In a saucepan, combine the granulated sugar and water. Heat over medium heat, stirring occasionally, until the sugar is completely dissolved to make a simple syrup.
2. Remove the syrup from heat and let it cool to room temperature.
3. In a mixing bowl, combine the freshly squeezed orange juice, orange zest, and lemon juice.
4. Stir in the cooled simple syrup and mix well.
5. Pour the mixture into an empty tub.
6. Place the lid on the tub and freeze for 24 hours.
7. After freezing, remove the tub from the freezer, assemble, and select the SORBET program.
8. Once processing is complete, Orange Sorbet is ready to serve.

Per Serving

Calories: 120; Fat: 0g;
Carbohydrates: 30g; Protein: 1g

CHAPTER 02: SORBET

Kiwi Sorbet

Serves: 6 ; Prep: 20 Min

Ingredient

- 500g kiwi fruit, peeled and chopped
- 100g granulated sugar
- 250ml water
- Juice of 1 lemon

Instruction:

1. In a saucepan, combine the granulated sugar and water. Heat over medium heat, stirring occasionally, until the sugar is completely dissolved to make a simple syrup.
2. Remove the syrup from heat and let it cool to room temperature.
3. In a blender, combine the chopped kiwi fruit and lemon juice. Blend until smooth.
4. Strain the kiwi puree through a fine mesh sieve to remove any seeds.
5. Stir in the cooled simple syrup and mix well.
6. Pour the mixture into an empty tub.
7. Place the lid on the tub and freeze for 24 hours.
8. After freezing, remove the tub from the freezer, assemble, and select the SORBET program.
9. Once processing is complete, Kiwi Sorbet is ready to serve.

Per Serving

Calories: 120; Fat: 0g;
Carbohydrates: 30g; Protein: 1g

Grapefruit Sorbet

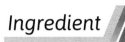 **Serves: 6 ; Prep: 30 Min**

Ingredient

- 4 large grapefruits
- 150g granulated sugar
- 250ml water
- Juice of 1 lemon

 Instruction:

1. Squeeze the juice from the grapefruits and strain it to remove any pulp or seeds.
2. In a saucepan, combine the granulated sugar and water. Heat over medium heat, stirring occasionally, until the sugar is completely dissolved to make a simple syrup.
3. Remove the syrup from heat and let it cool to room temperature.
4. In a blender, combine the grapefruit juice and lemon juice.
5. Stir in the cooled simple syrup and mix well.
6. Pour the mixture into an empty tub.
7. Place the lid on the tub and freeze for 24 hours.
8. After freezing, remove the tub from the freezer, assemble, and select the SORBET program.
9. Once processing is complete, Grapefruit Sorbet is ready to serve.

Per Serving

Calories: 120; Fat: 0g;
Carbohydrates: 30g; Protein: 1g

CHAPTER 02: SORBET

Coconut Sorbet

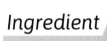 **Serves: 4 ; Prep: 15 Min**

Ingredient

- 400ml coconut milk
- 100g granulated sugar
- Juice of 1 lime

 Instruction:

1. In a saucepan, combine the coconut milk and granulated sugar.
2. Heat the mixture over medium heat, stirring constantly, until the sugar is completely dissolved. Remove from heat.
3. Let the mixture cool to room temperature.
4. Once cooled, stir in the lime juice until well combined.
5. Pour the mixture into an empty tub.
6. Place the lid on the tub and freeze for 24 hours.
7. After freezing, remove the tub from the freezer, assemble, and select the SORBET program.
8. Once processing is complete, Coconut Sorbet is ready to serve.

Per Serving

Calories: 200; Fat: 15g;
Carbohydrates: 20g; Protein: 1g

Cherry Sorbet

Serves: 4 ; Prep: 20 Min

Ingredient

- 500g fresh cherries, pitted
- 100g granulated sugar
- Juice of 1 lemon
- 100ml water

Instruction:

1. In a saucepan, combine the pitted cherries, granulated sugar, lemon juice, and water.
2. Heat the mixture over medium heat, stirring occasionally, until the cherries soften and the sugar is completely dissolved. Remove from heat and let it cool.
3. Once cooled, transfer the mixture to a blender and blend until smooth.
4. Strain the mixture through a fine mesh sieve to remove any solids.
5. Pour the cherry mixture into an empty tub.
6. Place the lid on the tub and freeze for 24 hours.
7. After freezing, remove the tub from the freezer, assemble, and select the SORBET program.
8. Once processing is complete, Cherry Sorbet is ready to serve.

Per Serving

Calories: 150; Fat: 0g;
Carbohydrates: 38g; Protein: 1g

CHAPTER 02: SORBET

Passion Fruit Sorbet

Serves: 4 ; Prep: 20 Min

Ingredient

- 300ml passion fruit juice (strained if necessary)
- 100g granulated sugar
- Juice of 1 lime
- Zest of 1 lime
- 100ml water

Instruction:

1. In a saucepan, combine the passion fruit juice, granulated sugar, lime juice, lime zest, and water.
2. Heat the mixture over medium heat, stirring occasionally, until the sugar is completely dissolved. Remove from heat and let it cool.
3. Once cooled, transfer the mixture to a blender and blend until smooth.
4. Pour the passion fruit mixture into an empty tub.
5. Place the lid on the tub and freeze for 24 hours.
6. After freezing, remove the tub from the freezer, assemble, and select the SORBET program.
7. Once processing is complete, Passion Fruit Sorbet is ready to serve.

Per Serving

Calories: 120; Fat: 0g;
Carbohydrates: 30g; Protein: 1g

Pomegranate Sorbet

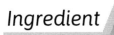 Serves: 4 ; Prep: 20 Min

 Ingredient

- 300ml pomegranate juice
- 100g granulated sugar
- Juice of 1 lemon
- Zest of 1 lemon
- 100ml water

Instruction:

1. In a saucepan, combine the pomegranate juice, granulated sugar, lemon juice, lemon zest, and water.
2. Heat the mixture over medium heat, stirring occasionally, until the sugar is completely dissolved. Remove from heat and let it cool.
3. Once cooled, transfer the mixture to a blender and blend until smooth.
4. Pour the pomegranate mixture into an empty tub.
5. Place the lid on the tub and freeze for 24 hours.
6. After freezing, remove the tub from the freezer, assemble, and select the SORBET program.
7. Once processing is complete, Pomegranate Sorbet is ready to serve.

Per Serving

Calories: 120; Fat: 0g;
Carbohydrates: 30g; Protein: 1g

CHAPTER 02: SORBET

Cranberry Sorbet

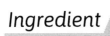 Serves: 4 ; Prep: 15 Min

 Ingredient

- 300g fresh cranberries
- 200g granulated sugar
- 240ml water
- Juice of 1 lemon

Instruction:

1. In a saucepan, combine the fresh cranberries, granulated sugar, water, and lemon juice.
2. Heat the mixture over medium heat, stirring occasionally, until the cranberries burst and the sugar is completely dissolved.
3. Remove from heat and let it cool to room temperature.
4. Once cooled, transfer the mixture to a blender and blend until smooth.
5. Pour the cranberry mixture into an empty tub.
6. Place the lid on the tub and freeze for 24 hours.
7. After freezing, remove the tub from the freezer, assemble, and select the SORBET program.
8. Once processing is complete, Cranberry Sorbet is ready to serve.

Per Serving

Calories: 170; Fat: 0g;
Carbohydrates: 44g; Protein: 0g

Green Apple Sorbet

Serves: 4 ; **Prep: 20 Min**

Ingredient

- 500g green apples, peeled, cored, and chopped
- 150g granulated sugar
- 240ml water
- Juice of 1 lemon

Per Serving

Calories: 180; Fat: 0g;
Carbohydrates: 47g; Protein: 0g

Instruction:

1. In a saucepan, combine the chopped green apples, granulated sugar, water, and lemon juice.
2. Heat the mixture over medium heat, stirring occasionally, until the apples are tender and the sugar is completely dissolved.
3. Remove from heat and let it cool to room temperature.
4. Once cooled, transfer the mixture to a blender and blend until smooth.
5. Pour the green apple mixture into an empty tub.
6. Place the lid on the tub and freeze for 24 hours.
7. After freezing, remove the tub from the freezer, assemble, and select the SORBET program.
8. Once processing is complete, Green Apple Sorbet is ready to serve.

CHAPTER 02: SORBET

Pear Sorbet

Serves: 4 ; **Prep: 20 Min**

Ingredient

- 500g ripe pears, peeled, cored, and diced
- 150g granulated sugar
- 240ml water
- Juice of 1 lemon

Per Serving

Calories: 180; Fat: 0g;
Carbohydrates: 47g; Protein: 0g

Instruction:

1. In a saucepan, combine the diced pears, granulated sugar, water, and lemon juice.
2. Heat the mixture over medium heat, stirring occasionally, until the pears are tender and the sugar is completely dissolved.
3. Remove from heat and let it cool to room temperature.
4. Once cooled, transfer the mixture to a blender and blend until smooth.
5. Pour the pear mixture into an empty tub.
6. Place the lid on the tub and freeze for 24 hours.
7. After freezing, remove the tub from the freezer, assemble, and select the SORBET program.
8. Once processing is complete, Pear Sorbet is ready to serve.

Plum Sorbet

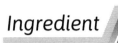 Serves: 4 ; Prep: 20 Min

Ingredient

- 500g ripe plums, pitted and halved
- 100g granulated sugar
- 240ml water
- Juice of 1 lemon

Instruction:

1. In a saucepan, combine the halved plums, granulated sugar, water, and lemon juice.
2. Heat the mixture over medium heat, stirring occasionally, until the plums are tender and the sugar is completely dissolved.
3. Remove from heat and let it cool to room temperature.
4. Once cooled, transfer the mixture to a blender and blend until smooth.
5. Pour the plum mixture into an empty tub.
6. Place the lid on the tub and freeze for 24 hours.
7. After freezing, remove the tub from the freezer, assemble, and select the SORBET program.
8. Once processing is complete, Plum Sorbet is ready to serve.

Per Serving

Calories: 120; Fat: 0g;
Carbohydrates: 31g; Protein: 0g

CHAPTER 02: SORBET

Apricot Sorbet

Serves: 4 ; Prep: 20 Min

Ingredient

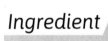

- 500g ripe apricots, halved and pitted
- 100g granulated sugar
- 240ml water
- Juice of 1 lemon

Instruction:

1. In a saucepan, combine the halved and pitted apricots, granulated sugar, water, and lemon juice.
2. Heat the mixture over medium heat, stirring occasionally, until the apricots are tender and the sugar is completely dissolved.
3. Remove from heat and let it cool to room temperature.
4. Once cooled, transfer the mixture to a blender and blend until smooth.
5. Pour the apricot mixture into an empty tub.
6. Place the lid on the tub and freeze for 24 hours.
7. After freezing, remove the tub from the freezer, assemble, and select the SORBET program.
8. Once processing is complete, Apricot Sorbet is ready to serve.

Per Serving

Calories: 110; Fat: 0g;
Carbohydrates: 28g; Protein: 1g

Guava Sorbet

 Serves: 4 ; Prep: 20 Min

Ingredient

- 500g ripe guavas, peeled and seeded
- 100g granulated sugar
- 240ml water
- Juice of 1 lime

 **Instruction:**

1. In a saucepan, combine the peeled and seeded guavas, granulated sugar, water, and lime juice.
2. Heat the mixture over medium heat, stirring occasionally, until the guavas are tender and the sugar is completely dissolved.
3. Remove from heat and let it cool to room temperature.
4. Once cooled, transfer the mixture to a blender and blend until smooth.
5. Pour the guava mixture into an empty tub.
6. Place the lid on the tub and freeze for 24 hours.
7. After freezing, remove the tub from the freezer, assemble, and select the SORBET program.
8. Once processing is complete, Guava Sorbet is ready to serve.

Per Serving

Calories: 120; Fat: 0g;
Carbohydrates: 30g; Protein: 1g

CHAPTER 02: SORBET

Lychee Sorbet

 Serves: 4 ; Prep: 20 Min

Ingredient
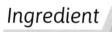

- 500g fresh lychees, peeled and deseeded
- 100g granulated sugar
- 240ml water
- Juice of 1 lime

Instruction:

1. In a saucepan, combine the peeled and deseeded lychees, granulated sugar, water, and lime juice.
2. Heat the mixture over medium heat, stirring occasionally, until the lychees are tender and the sugar is completely dissolved.
3. Remove from heat and let it cool to room temperature.
4. Once cooled, transfer the mixture to a blender and blend until smooth.
5. Pour the lychee mixture into an empty tub.
6. Place the lid on the tub and freeze for 24 hours.
7. After freezing, remove the tub from the freezer, assemble, and select the SORBET program.
8. Once processing is complete, Lychee Sorbet is ready to serve.

Per Serving

Calories: 120; Fat: 0g;
Carbohydrates: 30g; Protein: 1g

Papaya Sorbet

 **Serves: 4 ; Prep: 20 Min**

Ingredient

- 500g ripe papaya, peeled and seeds removed
- 100g granulated sugar
- 240ml water
- Juice of 1 lime

 ## Instruction:

1. Cut the ripe papaya into chunks and place them in a blender.
2. Add granulated sugar, water, and lime juice to the blender.
3. Blend until smooth.
4. Pour the mixture into a saucepan and heat over medium heat, stirring occasionally, until the sugar is completely dissolved.
5. Remove from heat and let it cool to room temperature.
6. Once cooled, pour the mixture into an empty tub.
7. Place the lid on the tub and freeze for 24 hours.
8. After freezing, remove the tub from the freezer, assemble, and select the SORBET program.
9. Once processing is complete, Papaya Sorbet is ready to serve.

Per Serving

Calories: 120; Fat: 0g;
Carbohydrates: 30g; Protein: 1g

CHAPTER 02: SORBET

Blood Orange Sorbet

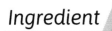 **Serves: 6 ; Prep: 15 Min**

Ingredient

- 400ml freshly squeezed blood orange juice (about 8 blood oranges)
- 150g granulated sugar
- 240ml water
- Zest of 1 blood orange
- Juice of 1 lemon

 ## Instruction:

1. In a saucepan, combine the granulated sugar, water, blood orange zest, and lemon juice. Bring to a simmer over medium heat, stirring until the sugar is completely dissolved.
2. Remove the syrup from heat and let it cool to room temperature.
3. Once cooled, stir in the freshly squeezed blood orange juice.
4. Pour the mixture into an empty tub.
5. Place the lid on the tub and freeze for 24 hours.
6. After freezing, remove the tub from the freezer, assemble, and select the SORBET program.
7. Once processing is complete, Blood Orange Sorbet is ready to serve.

Per Serving

Calories: 120; Fat: 0g;
Carbohydrates: 30g; Protein: 0g

Cantaloupe Sorbet

Serves: 6 ; Prep: 10 Min

Ingredient

- 1 ripe cantaloupe, peeled, seeded, and cubed
- 100g granulated sugar
- Juice of 1 lemon

Instruction:

1. Place the cubed cantaloupe in a blender or food processor.
2. Add the granulated sugar and lemon juice.
3. Blend until smooth.
4. Pour the mixture into an empty tub.
5. Place the lid on the tub and freeze for 24 hours.
6. After freezing, remove the tub from the freezer, assemble, and select the SORBET program.
7. Once processing is complete, Cantaloupe Sorbet is ready to serve.

Per Serving

Calories: 90; Fat: 0g;
Carbohydrates: 23g; Protein: Ig

CHAPTER 02: SORBET

Honeydew Sorbet

Serves: 6 ; Prep: 10 Min

Ingredient

- 1 honeydew melon, peeled, seeded, and cubed
- 100g granulated sugar
- Juice of 1 lime

Instruction:

1. Place the cubed honeydew melon in a blender or food processor.
2. Add the granulated sugar and lime juice.
3. Blend until smooth.
4. Pour the mixture into an empty tub.
5. Place the lid on the tub and freeze for 24 hours.
6. After freezing, remove the tub from the freezer, assemble, and select the SORBET program.
7. Once processing is complete, Honeydew Sorbet is ready to serve.

Per Serving

Calories: 90; Fat: 0g;
Carbohydrates: 23g; Protein: Ig

Tangerine Sorbet

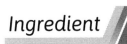 Serves: 6 ; Prep: 15 Min

Ingredient

- 500ml tangerine juice (from about 8-10 tangerines)
- 100g granulated sugar
- Zest of 1 tangerine
- Juice of 1 lemon

 ## Instruction:

1. In a saucepan, combine the tangerine juice, granulated sugar, tangerine zest, and lemon juice.
2. Heat over medium heat, stirring until the sugar is completely dissolved.
3. Remove from heat and let it cool to room temperature.
4. Pour the mixture into an empty tub.
5. Place the lid on the tub and freeze for 24 hours.
6. After freezing, remove the tub from the freezer, assemble, and select the SORBET program.
7. Once processing is complete, Tangerine Sorbet is ready to serve.

Per Serving

Calories: 120; Fat: 0g;
Carbohydrates: 30g; Protein: 0.5g

CHAPTER 02: SORBET

Raspberry Lime Sorbet

 Serves: 6 ; Prep: 15 Min

Ingredient

- 300g fresh raspberries
- Zest and juice of 2 limes
- 150g caster sugar
- 250ml water

Instruction:

1. In a saucepan, combine the raspberries, lime zest, lime juice, caster sugar, and water.
2. Heat over medium heat, stirring occasionally, until the sugar is dissolved and the raspberries break down, about 5-7 minutes.
3. Remove from heat and let it cool to room temperature.
4. Strain the mixture through a fine-mesh sieve to remove the seeds, pressing down to extract as much liquid as possible.
5. Pour the strained mixture into an empty tub.
6. Place the lid on the tub and freeze for 24 hours.
7. After freezing, remove the tub from the freezer, assemble, and select the SORBET program.
8. Once processing is complete, Raspberry Lime Sorbet is ready to serve.

Per Serving

Calories: 110; Fat: 0g;
Carbohydrates: 28g; Protein: 1g

Vanilla Bean Light Ice Cream

Serves: 6 ; Prep: 10 Min

Ingredient

- 225 ml double cream
- 140 ml semi-skimmed milk
- 1 vanilla bean, split and seeds scraped
- 2 tablespoons erythritol
- 2 tablespoons light agave syrup

 **Instruction:**

1. In a large bowl, combine double cream, semi-skimmed milk, vanilla bean seeds, erythritol, and light agave syrup.
2. Whisk the ingredients until well combined.
3. Pour the base into an empty tub. Place the lid on the tub and freeze for 24 hours.
4. Remove the tub from the freezer and take off the lid. Follow the quick instructions for assembly and processing.
5. Select the "LIGHT ICE CREAM" program.
6. Once processing is complete, add any desired mix-ins or serve the ice cream immediately.

Per Serving

Calories: 110; Fat: 9g;
Carbohydrates: 5g; Protein: 2g

CHAPTER 03: LIGHT ICE CREAM

Chocolate Light Ice Cream

Serves: 6 ; Prep: 10 Min

Ingredient

- 225 ml double cream
- 140 ml semi-skimmed milk
- 30 grams unsweetened cocoa powder
- 2 tablespoons erythritol
- 2 tablespoons light agave syrup

 Instruction:

1. In a large bowl, combine double cream, semi-skimmed milk, unsweetened cocoa powder, erythritol, and light agave syrup.
2. Whisk the ingredients until well combined.
3. Pour the base into an empty tub. Place the lid on the tub and freeze for 24 hours.
4. Remove the tub from the freezer and take off the lid. Follow the quick instructions for assembly and processing.
5. Select the "LIGHT ICE CREAM" program.
6. Once processing is complete, add any desired mix-ins or serve the ice cream immediately.

Per Serving

Calories: 120; Fat: 10g;
Carbohydrates: 5g; Protein: 2g

Strawberry
Light Ice Cream

Serves: 6 ; Prep: 10 Min

Ingredient

- 225 ml double cream
- 140 ml semi-skimmed milk
- 200 grams fresh strawberries, hulled and chopped
- 2 tablespoons erythritol
- 2 tablespoons light agave syrup

Per Serving

Calories: 110; Fat: 9g;
Carbohydrates: 6g; Protein: 2g

 ## Instruction:

1. In a large bowl, combine double cream, semi-skimmed milk, chopped fresh strawberries, erythritol, and light agave syrup.
2. Whisk the ingredients until well combined.
3. Pour the base into an empty tub. Place the lid on the tub and freeze for 24 hours.
4. Remove the tub from the freezer and take off the lid. Follow the quick instructions for assembly and processing.
5. Select the "LIGHT ICE CREAM" program.
6. Once processing is complete, add any desired mix-ins or serve the ice cream immediately.

CHAPTER 03: LIGHT ICE CREAM

Mint Chip
Light Ice Cream

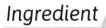
Serves: 6 ; Prep: 15 Min

Ingredient

- 225 ml double cream
- 140 ml semi-skimmed milk
- 1 teaspoon peppermint extract
- 50 grams dark chocolate, chopped into small pieces
- 2 tablespoons erythritol
- 2 tablespoons light agave syrup

Per Serving

Calories: 120; Fat: 9g;
Carbohydrates: 7g; Protein: 2g

Instruction:

1. In a large bowl, combine double cream, semi-skimmed milk, peppermint extract, chopped dark chocolate, erythritol, and light agave syrup.
2. Whisk the ingredients until well combined.
3. Pour the base into an empty tub. Place the lid on the tub and freeze for 24 hours.
4. Remove the tub from the freezer and take off the lid. Follow the quick instructions for assembly and processing.
5. Select the "LIGHT ICE CREAM" program.
6. Once processing is complete, add any desired mix-ins or serve the ice cream immediately.

Cookies and Cream Light Ice Cream

Serves: 6 ; Prep: 15 Min

Ingredient

- 225 ml double cream
- 140 ml semi-skimmed milk
- 100 grams chocolate sandwich cookies, crushed into small pieces
- 2 tablespoons erythritol
- 2 tablespoons light agave syrup

Per Serving

Calories: 130; Fat: 10g;
Carbohydrates: 8g; Protein: 2g

Instruction:

1. In a large bowl, combine double cream, semi-skimmed milk, crushed chocolate sandwich cookies, erythritol, and light agave syrup.
2. Whisk the ingredients until well combined.
3. Pour the base into an empty tub. Place the lid on the tub and freeze for 24 hours.
4. Remove the tub from the freezer and take off the lid. Follow the quick instructions for assembly and processing.
5. Select the "LIGHT ICE CREAM" program.
6. Once processing is complete, add any desired mix-ins or serve the ice cream immediately.

CHAPTER 03: LIGHT ICE CREAM

Coffee Light Ice Cream

Serves: 6 ; Prep: 10 Min

Ingredient

- 225 ml double cream
- 140 ml semi-skimmed milk
- 2 tablespoons instant coffee granules
- 2 tablespoons erythritol
- 2 tablespoons light agave syrup

Per Serving

Calories: 110; Fat: 9g;
Carbohydrates: 5g; Protein: 2g

Instruction:

1. In a large bowl, combine double cream, semi-skimmed milk, instant coffee granules, erythritol, and light agave syrup.
2. Whisk the ingredients until well combined.
3. Pour the base into an empty tub. Place the lid on the tub and freeze for 24 hours.
4. Remove the tub from the freezer and take off the lid. Follow the quick instructions for assembly and processing.
5. Select the "LIGHT ICE CREAM" program.
6. Once processing is complete, add any desired mix-ins or serve the ice cream immediately.

Peanut Butter Light Ice Cream

 Serves: 6 ; Prep: 15 Min

Ingredient

- 225 ml double cream
- 140 ml semi-skimmed milk
- 60 grams smooth peanut butter
- 2 tablespoons erythritol
- 2 tablespoons light agave syrup

 Instruction:

1. In a large bowl, combine double cream, semi-skimmed milk, smooth peanut butter, erythritol, and light agave syrup.
2. Whisk the ingredients until well combined.
3. Pour the base into an empty tub. Place the lid on the tub and freeze for 24 hours.
4. Remove the tub from the freezer and take off the lid. Follow the quick instructions for assembly and processing.
5. Select the "LIGHT ICE CREAM" program.
6. Once processing is complete, add any desired mix-ins or serve the ice cream immediately.

Per Serving

Calories: 140; Fat: 12g;
Carbohydrates: 6g; Protein: 3g

CHAPTER 03: LIGHT ICE CREAM

Almond Light Ice Cream

  Serves: 6 ; Prep: 10 Min

Ingredient

- 225 ml double cream
- 140 ml semi-skimmed milk
- 30 grams almond butter
- 2 tablespoons erythritol
- 2 tablespoons light agave syrup

Instruction:

1. In a large bowl, combine double cream, semi-skimmed milk, almond butter, erythritol, and light agave syrup.
2. Whisk the ingredients until well combined.
3. Pour the base into an empty tub. Place the lid on the tub and freeze for 24 hours.
4. Remove the tub from the freezer and take off the lid. Follow the quick instructions for assembly and processing.
5. Select the "LIGHT ICE CREAM" program.
6. Once processing is complete, add any desired mix-ins or serve the ice cream immediately.

Per Serving

Calories: 130; Fat: 10g;
Carbohydrates: 6g; Protein: 2g

Raspberry Light Ice Cream

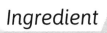

Serves: 6 ; Prep: 15 Min

Ingredient

- 225 ml double cream
- 140 ml semi-skimmed milk
- 150 grams fresh raspberries
- 2 tablespoons erythritol
- 2 tablespoons light agave syrup

<u>Per Serving</u>

Calories: 110; Fat: 9g;
Carbohydrates: 6g; Protein: 2g

Instruction:

1. In a large bowl, combine double cream, semi-skimmed milk, fresh raspberries, erythritol, and light agave syrup.
2. Whisk the ingredients until well combined.
3. Pour the base into an empty tub. Place the lid on the tub and freeze for 24 hours.
4. Remove the tub from the freezer and take off the lid. Follow the quick instructions for assembly and processing.
5. Select the "LIGHT ICE CREAM" program.
6. Once processing is complete, add any desired mix-ins or serve the ice cream immediately.

Coconut Light Ice Cream

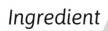

Serves: 6 ; Prep: 10 Min

Ingredient

- 225 ml double cream
- 140 ml semi-skimmed milk
- 50 grams desiccated coconut
- 2 tablespoons erythritol
- 2 tablespoons light agave syrup

<u>Per Serving</u>

Calories: 130; Fat: 10g;
Carbohydrates: 6g; Protein: 2g

Instruction:

1. In a large bowl, combine double cream, semi-skimmed milk, desiccated coconut, erythritol, and light agave syrup.
2. Whisk the ingredients until well combined.
3. Pour the base into an empty tub. Place the lid on the tub and freeze for 24 hours.
4. Remove the tub from the freezer and take off the lid. Follow the quick instructions for assembly and processing.
5. Select the "LIGHT ICE CREAM" program.
6. Once processing is complete, add any desired mix-ins or serve the ice cream immediately.

Banana Light Ice Cream

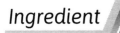 Serves: 6 ; Prep: 10 Min

Ingredient

- 225 ml double cream
- 140 ml semi-skimmed milk
- 2 ripe bananas, mashed
- 2 tablespoons erythritol
- 2 tablespoons light agave syrup

Per Serving

Calories: 120; Fat: 9g;
Carbohydrates: 7g; Protein: 2g

 Instruction:

1. Combine double cream, semi-skimmed milk, mashed bananas, erythritol, and light agave syrup in a large bowl.
2. Whisk the ingredients until well combined.
3. Pour the mixture into an empty tub. Place the lid on the tub and freeze for 24 hours.
4. After freezing, remove the tub from the freezer and take off the lid. Follow the quick instructions for assembly and processing.
5. Select the "LIGHT ICE CREAM" program.
6. Once the processing is complete, add any desired mix-ins or serve the ice cream immediately.

CHAPTER 03: LIGHT ICE CREAM

Lemon Light Ice Cream

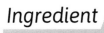 Serves: 6 ; Prep: 10 Min

Ingredient

- 225 ml double cream
- 140 ml semi-skimmed milk
- Zest of 2 lemons
- Juice of 2 lemons
- 2 tablespoons erythritol
- 2 tablespoons light agave syrup

Per Serving

Calories: 110; Fat: 9g;
Carbohydrates: 6g; Protein: 2g

Instruction:

1. In a large bowl, combine double cream, semi-skimmed milk, lemon zest, lemon juice, erythritol, and light agave syrup.
2. Whisk the ingredients until well combined.
3. Pour the mixture into an empty tub. Place the lid on the tub and freeze for 24 hours.
4. After freezing, remove the tub from the freezer and take off the lid. Follow the quick instructions for assembly and processing.
5. Select the "LIGHT ICE CREAM" program.
6. Once the processing is complete, add any desired mix-ins or serve the ice cream immediately.

Blueberry Light Ice Cream

Serves: 6 ; Prep: 15 Min

 Ingredient

- 225 ml double cream
- 140 ml semi-skimmed milk
- 150 grams fresh blueberries
- 2 tablespoons erythritol
- 2 tablespoons light agave syrup

<u>Per Serving</u>

Calories: 110; Fat: 9g;
Carbohydrates: 6g; Protein: 2g

 Instruction:

1. In a large bowl, combine double cream, semi-skimmed milk, fresh blueberries, erythritol, and light agave syrup.
2. Whisk the ingredients until well combined.
3. Pour the mixture into an empty tub. Place the lid on the tub and freeze for 24 hours.
4. After freezing, remove the tub from the freezer and take off the lid. Follow the quick instructions for assembly and processing.
5. Select the "LIGHT ICE CREAM" program.
6. Once the processing is complete, add any desired mix-ins or serve the ice cream immediately.

CHAPTER 03: LIGHT ICE CREAM

Mango Light Ice Cream

Serves: 6 ; Prep: 15 Min

 Ingredient

- 225 ml double cream
- 140 ml semi-skimmed milk
- 2 ripe mangoes, peeled and diced
- 2 tablespoons erythritol
- 2 tablespoons light agave syrup

<u>Per Serving</u>

Calories: 120; Fat: 9g;
Carbohydrates: 7g; Protein: 2g

Instruction:

1. In a large bowl, combine double cream, semi-skimmed milk, diced mangoes, erythritol, and light agave syrup.
2. Whisk the ingredients until well combined.
3. Pour the mixture into an empty tub. Place the lid on the tub and freeze for 24 hours.
4. After freezing, remove the tub from the freezer and take off the lid. Follow the quick instructions for assembly and processing.
5. Select the "LIGHT ICE CREAM" program.
6. Once the processing is complete, add any desired mix-ins or serve the ice cream immediately.

Peach Light Ice Cream

 Serves: 6 ; Prep: 15 Min

Ingredient

- 225 ml double cream
- 140 ml semi-skimmed milk
- 2 ripe peaches, peeled and diced
- 2 tablespoons erythritol
- 2 tablespoons light agave syrup

Per Serving

Calories: 120; Fat: 9g;
Carbohydrates: 7g; Protein: 2g

Instruction:

1. In a large bowl, combine double cream, semi-skimmed milk, diced peaches, erythritol, and light agave syrup.
2. Whisk the ingredients until well combined.
3. Pour the mixture into an empty tub. Place the lid on the tub and freeze for 24 hours.
4. After freezing, remove the tub from the freezer and take off the lid. Follow the quick instructions for assembly and processing.
5. Select the "LIGHT ICE CREAM" program.
6. Once the processing is complete, add any desired mix-ins or serve the ice cream immediately.

CHAPTER 03: LIGHT ICE CREAM

Pineapple Light Ice Cream

 Serves: 6 ; Prep: 15 Min

Ingredient

- 225 ml double cream
- 140 ml semi-skimmed milk
- 160g diced pineapple
- 2 tablespoons erythritol
- 2 tablespoons light agave syrup

Per Serving

Calories: 110; Fat: 9g;
Carbohydrates: 7g; Protein: 2g

Instruction:

1. In a large bowl, combine double cream, semi-skimmed milk, diced pineapple, erythritol, and light agave syrup.
2. Whisk the ingredients until well combined.
3. Pour the mixture into an empty tub. Place the lid on the tub and freeze for 24 hours.
4. After freezing, remove the tub from the freezer and take off the lid. Follow the quick instructions for assembly and processing.
5. Select the "LIGHT ICE CREAM" program.
6. Once the processing is complete, add any desired mix-ins or serve the ice cream immediately.

Blackberry Light Ice Cream

Serves: 6 ; **Prep: 15 Min**

Ingredient

- 225 ml double cream
- 140 ml semi-skimmed milk
- 140g blackberries
- 2 tablespoons stevia granules
- 2 tablespoons light agave syrup

Per Serving

Calories: 100; Fat: 7g;
Carbohydrates: 8g; Protein: 2g

 **Instruction:**

1. In a large bowl, combine double cream, semi-skimmed milk, blackberries, stevia granules, and light agave syrup.
2. Whisk the ingredients until well combined.
3. Pour the mixture into an empty tub. Place the lid on the tub and freeze for 24 hours.
4. After freezing, remove the tub from the freezer and take off the lid. Follow the quick instructions for assembly and processing.
5. Select the "LIGHT ICE CREAM" program.
6. Once the processing is complete, add any desired mix-ins or serve the ice cream immediately.

CHAPTER 03: LIGHT ICE CREAM

Orange Light Ice Cream

Serves: 6 ; **Prep: 15 Min**

Ingredient

- 225 ml double cream
- 140 ml semi-skimmed milk
- Zest of 1 orange
- 2 tablespoons orange juice
- 2 tablespoons stevia granules
- 2 tablespoons light agave syrup

Per Serving

Calories: 110; Fat: 8g;
Carbohydrates: 9g; Protein: 2g

 Instruction:

1. In a large bowl, combine double cream, semi-skimmed milk, orange zest, orange juice, stevia granules, and light agave syrup.
2. Whisk the ingredients until well combined.
3. Pour the mixture into an empty tub. Place the lid on the tub and freeze for 24 hours.
4. After freezing, remove the tub from the freezer and take off the lid. Follow the quick instructions for assembly and processing.
5. Select the "LIGHT ICE CREAM" program.
6. Once the processing is complete, add any desired mix-ins or serve the ice cream immediately.

Cherry Light Ice Cream

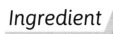 **Serves: 6 ; Prep: 15 Min**

Ingredient

- 225 ml double cream
- 140 ml semi-skimmed milk
- 200 g fresh cherries, pitted and chopped
- 2 tablespoons stevia granules
- 2 tablespoons light agave syrup

Per Serving

Calories: 120; Fat: 9g;
Carbohydrates: 10g; Protein: 2g

 ## Instruction:

1. Combine double cream, semi-skimmed milk, chopped cherries, stevia granules, and light agave syrup in a large bowl.
2. Whisk the ingredients until thoroughly combined.
3. Pour the mixture into an empty tub. Place the lid on the tub and freeze for 24 hours.
4. Remove the tub from the freezer and take off the lid. Follow the quick instructions for assembly and processing.
5. Select the "LIGHT ICE CREAM" program.
6. Once processing is complete, add any desired mix-ins or serve the ice cream immediately.

CHAPTER 03: LIGHT ICE CREAM

Pistachio Light Ice Cream

 **Serves: 6 ; Prep: 15 Min**

Ingredient

- 225 ml double cream
- 140 ml semi-skimmed milk
- 100 g shelled pistachios, finely chopped
- 2 tablespoons stevia granules
- 2 tablespoons light agave syrup

Per Serving

Calories: 150; Fat: 12g;
Carbohydrates: 8g; Protein: 3g

 ## Instruction:

1. In a large bowl, combine double cream, semi-skimmed milk, chopped pistachios, stevia granules, and light agave syrup.
2. Whisk the ingredients until well combined.
3. Pour the mixture into an empty tub. Place the lid on the tub and freeze for 24 hours.
4. Remove the tub from the freezer and take off the lid. Follow the quick instructions for assembly and processing.
5. Select the "LIGHT ICE CREAM" program.
6. Once processing is complete, add any desired mix-ins or serve the ice cream immediately.

Honey Light Ice Cream

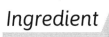

Serves: 6 ; Prep: 10 Min

Ingredient

- 225 ml double cream
- 140 ml semi-skimmed milk
- 4 tablespoons honey

Instruction:

1. In a large bowl, combine double cream, semi-skimmed milk, and honey.
2. Whisk the ingredients until well combined.
3. Pour the mixture into an empty tub. Place the lid on the tub and freeze for 24 hours.
4. Remove the tub from the freezer and take off the lid. Follow the quick instructions for assembly and processing.
5. Select the "LIGHT ICE CREAM" program.
6. Once processing is complete, add any desired mix-ins or serve the ice cream immediately.

Per Serving

Calories: 160; Fat: 12g;
Carbohydrates: 10g; Protein: 2g

CHAPTER 03: LIGHT ICE CREAM

Maple Light Ice Cream

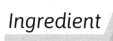

Serves: 6 ; Prep: 10 Min

Ingredient

- 225 ml double cream
- 140 ml semi-skimmed milk
- 4 tablespoons maple syrup

Instruction:

1. Combine double cream, semi-skimmed milk, and maple syrup in a large bowl.
2. Whisk until thoroughly mixed.
3. Pour the mixture into an empty tub. Seal with the lid and freeze for 24 hours.
4. Remove the tub from the freezer, take off the lid, and follow the quick instructions for assembly and processing.
5. Select the "LIGHT ICE CREAM" program on your Ninja CREAMi machine.
6. Once the processing is complete, you can add any desired mix-ins or serve the ice cream immediately.

Per Serving

Calories: 160; Fat: 12g;
Carbohydrates: 10g; Protein: 2g

Cinnamon
Light Ice Cream

Serves: 6 ; Prep: 10 Min

Ingredient

- 225 ml double cream
- 140 ml semi-skimmed milk
- 2 teaspoons ground cinnamon
- 2 tablespoons honey or maple syrup

Per Serving

Calories: 150; Fat: 10g;
Carbohydrates: 13g; Protein: 2g

Instruction:

1. Combine double cream, semi-skimmed milk, ground cinnamon, and honey/maple syrup in a large bowl.
2. Whisk until thoroughly mixed.
3. Pour the mixture into an empty tub. Seal with the lid and freeze for 24 hours.
4. Remove the tub from the freezer, take off the lid, and follow the quick instructions for assembly and processing.
5. Select the "LIGHT ICE CREAM" program on your Ninja CREAMi machine.
6. Once the processing is complete, you can add any desired mix-ins or serve the ice cream immediately.

CHAPTER 03: LIGHT ICE CREAM

Hazelnut
Light Ice Cream

Serves: 6 ; Prep: 10 Min

Ingredient

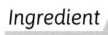 

- 225 ml double cream
- 140 ml semi-skimmed milk
- 50 grams hazelnuts, finely chopped or ground
- 2 tablespoons honey or maple syrup

Per Serving

Calories: 160; Fat: 11g;
Carbohydrates: 14g; Protein: 2g

Instruction:

1. Combine double cream, semi-skimmed milk, chopped or ground hazelnuts, and honey/maple syrup in a large bowl.
2. Whisk until thoroughly mixed.
3. Pour the mixture into an empty tub. Seal with the lid and freeze for 24 hours.
4. Remove the tub from the freezer, take off the lid, and follow the quick instructions for assembly and processing.
5. Select the "LIGHT ICE CREAM" program on your Ninja CREAMi machine.
6. Once the processing is complete, you can add any desired mix-ins or serve the ice cream immediately.

Vanilla Bean Gelato

 Serves: 6 ; Prep: 20 Min

Ingredient

- 3 large egg yolks
- 70g caster sugar
- 300ml double cream
- 250ml whole milk
- 2 vanilla beans, split lengthwise and seeds scraped out

Instruction:

1. In a small saucepan, whisk together the egg yolks and caster sugar until fully combined and the sugar is dissolved.
2. Add the double cream, whole milk, and scraped vanilla bean seeds to the saucepan, stirring to combine.
3. Place the saucepan on the hob over medium heat, stirring constantly with a whisk or silicone spatula. Cook until the temperature reaches 165-175°F (74-79°C) on an instant-read thermometer.
4. Remove the base from the heat and pour it through a fine-mesh sieve into an empty tub. Place the lid on the tub and freeze for at least 24 hours.
5. Remove the tub from the freezer and let it sit at room temperature for a few minutes. Remove the lid from the tub.
6. Select the "GELATO" program on your Ninja CREAMi.
7. Once processing is complete, add any mix-ins if desired, or serve the vanilla bean gelato immediately.

Per Serving

Calories: 270; Fat: 21g;
Carbohydrates: 17g; Protein: 4g

CHAPTER 04: GELATO

Chocolate Gelato

 Serves: 6 ; Prep: 20 Min

Ingredient

- 3 large egg yolks
- 70g caster sugar
- 300ml double cream
- 250ml whole milk
- 100g dark chocolate, chopped

Instruction:

1. In a small saucepan, whisk together the egg yolks and caster sugar until fully combined and the sugar is dissolved.
2. Add the double cream and whole milk to the saucepan, stirring to combine.
3. Place the saucepan on the hob over medium heat, stirring constantly with a whisk or silicone spatula. Cook until the temperature reaches 165-175°F (74-79°C) on an instant-read thermometer.
4. Remove the base from the heat and stir in the chopped dark chocolate until melted and smooth.
5. Pour the mixture through a fine-mesh sieve into an empty tub. Place the lid on the tub and freeze for at least 24 hours.
6. Remove the tub from the freezer and let it sit at room temperature for a few minutes. Remove the lid from the tub.
7. Select the "GELATO" program on your Ninja CREAMi.
8. Once processing is complete, serve the chocolate gelato immediately.

Per Serving

Calories: 320; Fat: 25g;
Carbohydrates: 20g; Protein: 5g

Strawberry Gelato

 Serves: 6 ; Prep: 20 Min

Ingredient

- 300g fresh strawberries, hulled and chopped
- 70g caster sugar
- 300ml double cream
- 250ml whole milk
- 1 teaspoon lemon juice

Per Serving

Calories: 220; Fat: 17g;
Carbohydrates: 16g; Protein: 3g

Instruction:

1. In a blender, combine the chopped strawberries and caster sugar. Blend until smooth.
2. In a small saucepan, whisk together the double cream and whole milk.
3. Add the blended strawberry mixture and lemon juice to the saucepan, stirring to combine.
4. Place the saucepan on the hob over medium heat, stirring constantly with a whisk or silicone spatula. Cook until the temperature reaches 165-175°F (74-79°C) on an instant-read thermometer.
5. Remove the base from the heat and pour it through a fine-mesh sieve into an empty tub. Place the lid on the tub and freeze for at least 24 hours.
6. Remove the tub from the freezer and let it sit at room temperature for a few minutes. Remove the lid from the tub.
7. Select the "GELATO" program on your Ninja CREAMi.
8. Once processing is complete, serve the strawberry gelato immediately.

CHAPTER 04: GELATO

Pistachio Gelato

 Serves: 6 ; Prep: 20 Min

Ingredient

- 100g shelled pistachio nuts
- 70g caster sugar
- 300ml double cream
- 250ml whole milk

Per Serving

Calories: 300; Fat: 24g;
Carbohydrates: 16g; Protein: 5g

Instruction:

1. In a food processor, pulse the shelled pistachio nuts until finely chopped.
2. In a small saucepan, whisk together the caster sugar, double cream, and whole milk.
3. Add the finely chopped pistachios to the saucepan, stirring to combine.
4. Place the saucepan on the hob over medium heat, stirring constantly with a whisk or silicone spatula. Cook until the temperature reaches 165-175°F (74-79°C) on an instant-read thermometer.
5. Remove the base from the heat and pour it through a fine-mesh sieve into an empty tub. Place the lid on the tub and freeze for at least 24 hours.
6. Remove the tub from the freezer and let it sit at room temperature for a few minutes. Remove the lid from the tub.
7. Select the "GELATO" program on your Ninja CREAMi.
8. Once processing is complete, serve the pistachio gelato immediately.

Hazelnut Gelato

 Serves: 6 ; Prep: 20 Min

Ingredient

- 100g hazelnuts
- 70g caster sugar
- 300ml double cream
- 250ml whole milk

Per Serving

Calories: 310; Fat: 25g;
Carbohydrates: 18g; Protein: 5g

Instruction:

1. Toast the hazelnuts in a dry pan over medium heat until lightly browned and fragrant, stirring frequently to prevent burning. Remove from heat and let them cool.
2. Once cooled, place the toasted hazelnuts in a food processor and blend until finely ground.
3. In a small saucepan, whisk together the caster sugar, double cream, and whole milk.
4. Add the finely ground hazelnuts to the saucepan, stirring to combine.
5. Place the saucepan on the hob over medium heat, stirring constantly with a whisk or silicone spatula. Cook until the temperature reaches 165-175°F (74-79°C) on an instant-read thermometer.
6. Remove the base from the heat and pour it through a fine-mesh sieve into an empty tub. Place the lid on the tub and freeze for at least 24 hours.
7. Remove the tub from the freezer and let it sit at room temperature for a few minutes. Remove the lid from the tub.
8. Select the "GELATO" program on your Ninja CREAMi.
9. Once processing is complete, serve the hazelnut gelato immediately.

CHAPTER 04: GELATO

Coffee Gelato

 Serves: 6 ; Prep: 20 Min

Ingredient

- 3 large egg yolks
- 80g caster sugar
- 200ml whipping cream
- 170ml whole milk
- 2 teaspoons instant espresso powder
- Pinch of salt

Per Serving

Calories: 210; Fat: 15g;
Carbohydrates: 15g; Protein: 3g

Instruction:

1. In a small saucepan, whisk together the egg yolks and caster sugar until fully combined and the sugar is dissolved.
2. Add the whipping cream, whole milk, instant espresso powder, and salt to the saucepan, stirring to combine.
3. Place the saucepan on the hob over medium heat, stirring constantly with a whisk or silicone spatula. Cook until the temperature reaches 165-175°F (74-79°C) on an instant-read thermometer.
4. Remove the base from the heat and pour it through a fine-mesh sieve into an empty tub. Place the lid on the tub and freeze for at least 24 hours.
5. Remove the tub from the freezer and let it sit at room temperature for a few minutes. Remove the lid from the tub.
6. Select the "GELATO" program on your Ninja CREAMi.
7. Once processing is complete, serve the coffee gelato immediately.

Mint Chocolate Chip Gelato

 Serves: 6 ; Prep: 20 Min

Ingredient

- 3 large egg yolks
- 80g caster sugar
- 200ml whipping cream
- 170ml whole milk
- 1 teaspoon peppermint extract
- 75g dark chocolate, chopped

Per Serving

Calories: 250; Fat: 18g;
Carbohydrates: 20g; Protein: 4g

Instruction:

1. In a small saucepan, whisk together the egg yolks and caster sugar until fully combined and the sugar is dissolved.
2. Add the whipping cream, whole milk, and peppermint extract to the saucepan, stirring to combine.
3. Place the saucepan on the hob over medium heat, stirring constantly with a whisk or silicone spatula. Cook until the temperature reaches 165-175°F (74-79°C) on an instant-read thermometer.
4. Remove the base from the heat and pour it through a fine-mesh sieve into an empty tub. Place the lid on the tub and freeze for at least 24 hours.
5. Remove the tub from the freezer and let it sit at room temperature for a few minutes. Remove the lid from the tub.
6. Select the "GELATO" program on your Ninja CREAMi.
7. Once processing is complete, add the chopped dark chocolate to the gelato and mix gently.
8. Serve the mint chocolate chip gelato immediately.

CHAPTER 04: GELATO

Cookies and Cream Gelato

 Serves: 6 ; Prep: 20 Min

Ingredient

- 3 large egg yolks
- 80g caster sugar
- 200ml whipping cream
- 170ml whole milk
- 100g chocolate cookies, crushed

Per Serving

Calories: 280; Fat: 20g;
Carbohydrates: 22g; Protein: 4g

Instruction:

1. In a small saucepan, whisk together the egg yolks and caster sugar until fully combined and the sugar is dissolved.
2. Add the whipping cream and whole milk to the saucepan, stirring to combine.
3. Place the saucepan on the hob over medium heat, stirring constantly with a whisk or silicone spatula. Cook until the temperature reaches 165-175°F (74-79°C) on an instant-read thermometer.
4. Remove the base from the heat and pour it through a fine-mesh sieve into an empty tub. Place the lid on the tub and freeze for at least 24 hours.
5. Remove the tub from the freezer and let it sit at room temperature for a few minutes. Remove the lid from the tub.
6. Select the "GELATO" program on your Ninja CREAMi.
7. Once processing is complete, add the crushed chocolate cookies to the gelato and mix gently.
8. Serve the cookies and cream gelato immediately.

Salted Caramel Gelato

Serves: 6 ; Prep: 20 Min

Ingredient

- 3 large egg yolks
- 80g caster sugar
- 200ml whipping cream
- 170ml whole milk
- 100g caramel sauce
- Pinch of sea salt

Per Serving

Calories: 280; Fat: 20g;
Carbohydrates: 22g; Protein: 4g

Instruction:

1. In a small saucepan, whisk together the egg yolks and caster sugar until fully combined and the sugar is dissolved.
2. Add the whipping cream and whole milk to the saucepan, stirring to combine.
3. Place the saucepan on the hob over medium heat, stirring constantly with a whisk or silicone spatula. Cook until the temperature reaches 165-175°F (74-79°C) on an instant-read thermometer.
4. Remove the base from the heat and stir in the caramel sauce and a pinch of sea salt until well combined.
5. Pour the mixture through a fine-mesh sieve into an empty tub. Place the lid on the tub and freeze for at least 24 hours.
6. Remove the tub from the freezer and let it sit at room temperature for a few minutes. Remove the lid from the tub.
7. Select the "GELATO" program on your Ninja CREAMi.
8. Once processing is complete, serve the salted caramel gelato immediately.

Tiramisu Gelato

Serves: 6 ; Prep: 20 Min

Ingredient

- 3 large egg yolks
- 80g caster sugar
- 200ml whipping cream
- 170ml whole milk
- 2 tablespoons instant coffee granules
- 2 tablespoons coffee liqueur (optional)
- 100g ladyfinger biscuits, crushed
- 25g cocoa powder

Per Serving

Calories: 280; Fat: 18g;
Carbohydrates: 23g; Protein: 4g

Instruction:

1. In a small saucepan, whisk together the egg yolks and caster sugar until fully combined and the sugar is dissolved.
2. Add the whipping cream, whole milk, instant coffee granules, and coffee liqueur (if using) to the saucepan, stirring to combine.
3. Place the saucepan on the hob over medium heat, stirring constantly with a whisk or silicone spatula. Cook until the temperature reaches 165-175°F (74-79°C) on an instant-read thermometer.
4. Remove the base from the heat and pour it through a fine-mesh sieve into an empty tub. Place the lid on the tub and freeze for at least 24 hours.
5. Remove the tub from the freezer and let it sit at room temperature for a few minutes. Remove the lid from the tub.
6. Select the "GELATO" program on your Ninja CREAMi.
7. Once processing is complete, add the crushed ladyfinger biscuits to the gelato and mix gently.
8. Serve the tiramisu gelato immediately, dusted with cocoa powder.

Mango Gelato

Serves: 6 ; Prep: 20 Min

Ingredient

- 3 large ripe mangoes, peeled and chopped
- 80g caster sugar
- 200ml whipping cream
- 170ml whole milk
- Juice of 1 lime

Instruction:

1. In a blender, combine the chopped mangoes, caster sugar, whipping cream, whole milk, and lime juice. Blend until smooth.
2. Pour the mango mixture into a small saucepan and heat gently over medium heat, stirring occasionally, until the sugar is dissolved and the mixture is warm.
3. Remove the saucepan from the heat and let the mixture cool to room temperature.
4. Pour the cooled mixture through a fine-mesh sieve into an empty tub. Place the lid on the tub and freeze for at least 24 hours.
5. Remove the tub from the freezer and let it sit at room temperature for a few minutes. Remove the lid from the tub.
6. Select the "GELATO" program on your Ninja CREAMi.
7. Once processing is complete, serve the mango gelato immediately.

Per Serving
Calories: 180; Fat: 10g;
Carbohydrates: 23g; Protein: 2g

CHAPTER 04: GELATO

Raspberry Gelato

Serves: 6 ; Prep: 20 Min

Ingredient

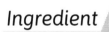

- 300g fresh raspberries
- 80g caster sugar
- 200ml whipping cream
- 170ml whole milk
- Juice of 1 lemon

Instruction:

1. In a blender, combine the fresh raspberries, caster sugar, whipping cream, whole milk, and lemon juice. Blend until smooth.
2. Pour the raspberry mixture into a small saucepan and heat gently over medium heat, stirring occasionally, until the sugar is dissolved and the mixture is warm.
3. Remove the saucepan from the heat and let the mixture cool to room temperature.
4. Pour the cooled mixture through a fine-mesh sieve into an empty tub. Place the lid on the tub and freeze for at least 24 hours.
5. Remove the tub from the freezer and let it sit at room temperature for a few minutes. Remove the lid from the tub.
6. Select the "GELATO" program on your Ninja CREAMi.
7. Once processing is complete, serve the raspberry gelato immediately.

Per Serving
Calories: 160; Fat: 10g;
Carbohydrates: 16g; Protein: 2g

Lemon Sorbetto Gelato

Serves: 6 ; Prep: 15 Min

Ingredient

- 250ml water
- 150g caster sugar
- Zest and juice of 2 lemons

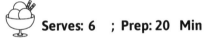

Instruction:

1. In a saucepan, combine water and caster sugar. Heat over medium heat, stirring occasionally, until the sugar is fully dissolved. Remove from heat.
2. Add the lemon zest and juice to the sugar syrup. Stir to combine.
3. Allow the mixture to cool to room temperature.
4. Once cooled, pour the lemon mixture into the Ninja CREAMi tub.
5. Place the lid on the tub and freeze for at least 24 hours.
6. Remove the tub from the freezer and let it sit at room temperature for a few minutes. Remove the lid from the tub.
7. Select the "GELATO" program on your Ninja CREAMi.
8. Once processing is complete, serve the lemon sorbetto gelato immediately.

Per Serving

Calories: 110; Fat: 0g;
Carbohydrates: 29g; Protein: 0g

CHAPTER 04: GELATO

Coconut Gelato

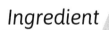

Serves: 6 ; Prep: 20 Min

Ingredient

- 400ml coconut milk
- 100g caster sugar
- 120ml coconut cream
- 1 teaspoon vanilla extract

Instruction:

1. In a saucepan, combine the coconut milk and caster sugar. Heat over medium heat, stirring occasionally, until the sugar is fully dissolved. Remove from heat.
2. Stir in the coconut cream and vanilla extract until well combined.
3. Allow the mixture to cool to room temperature.
4. Once cooled, pour the coconut mixture into the Ninja CREAMi tub.
5. Place the lid on the tub and freeze for at least 24 hours.
6. Remove the tub from the freezer and let it sit at room temperature for a few minutes. Remove the lid from the tub.
7. Select the "GELATO" program on your Ninja CREAMi.
8. Once processing is complete, serve the coconut gelato immediately.

Per Serving

Calories: 270; Fat: 21g;
Carbohydrates: 20g; Protein: 2g

Almond Gelato

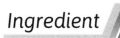 Serves: 6 ; Prep: 15 Min

Ingredient

- 500ml whole milk
- 100g caster sugar
- 100g ground almonds
- 1 teaspoon almond extract
- 100ml double cream

Instruction:

1. In a saucepan, combine the whole milk and caster sugar. Heat over medium heat, stirring occasionally, until the sugar is fully dissolved.
2. Stir in the ground almonds and almond extract until well combined.
3. Remove the mixture from heat and allow it to cool to room temperature.
4. Once cooled, stir in the double cream until smooth.
5. Pour the almond mixture into the Ninja CREAMi tub.
6. Place the lid on the tub and freeze for at least 24 hours.
7. Remove the tub from the freezer and let it sit at room temperature for a few minutes. Remove the lid from the tub.
8. Select the "GELATO" program on your Ninja CREAMi.
9. Once processing is complete, serve the almond gelato immediately.

Per Serving

Calories: 230; Fat: 14g;
Carbohydrates: 21g; Protein: 5g

CHAPTER 04: GELATO

Banana Gelato

 Serves: 4 ; Prep: 05 Min

Ingredient

- 4 ripe bananas
- 200ml whole milk
- 50g caster sugar
- 100ml double cream

Instruction:

1. Peel the ripe bananas and slice them into small pieces.
2. In a blender, combine the banana slices, whole milk, and caster sugar. Blend until smooth.
3. Pour the banana mixture into a saucepan and heat over low heat, stirring constantly, until the sugar is dissolved.
4. Remove the banana mixture from heat and allow it to cool to room temperature.
5. Once cooled, stir in the double cream until well combined.
6. Pour the banana mixture into the Ninja CREAMi tub.
7. Place the lid on the tub and freeze for at least 24 hours.
8. Remove the tub from the freezer and let it sit at room temperature for a few minutes. Remove the lid from the tub.
9. Select the "GELATO" program on your Ninja CREAMi.
10. Once processing is complete, serve the banana gelato immediately.

Per Serving

Calories: 210; Fat: 10g;
Carbohydrates: 31g; Protein: 2g

Cherry Gelato

 Serves: 4 ; Prep: 10 Min

Ingredient

- 400g fresh cherries, pitted
- 200ml whole milk
- 100g caster sugar
- 100ml double cream

Instruction:

1. Wash and pit the fresh cherries, then cut them into halves.
2. In a blender, combine the cherries, whole milk, and caster sugar. Blend until smooth.
3. Pour the cherry mixture into a saucepan and heat over low heat, stirring constantly, until the sugar is dissolved.
4. Remove the cherry mixture from heat and allow it to cool to room temperature.
5. Once cooled, stir in the double cream until well combined.
6. Pour the cherry mixture into the Ninja CREAMi tub.
7. Place the lid on the tub and freeze for at least 24 hours.
8. Remove the tub from the freezer and let it sit at room temperature for a few minutes. Remove the lid from the tub.
9. Select the "GELATO" program on your Ninja CREAMi.
10. Once processing is complete, serve the cherry gelato immediately.

Per Serving

Calories: 220; Fat: 9g;
Carbohydrates: 34g; Protein: 2g

CHAPTER 04: GELATO

Blueberry Gelato

 Serves: 4 ; Prep: 15 Min

Ingredient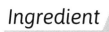

- 300g fresh blueberries
- 200ml whole milk
- 100g caster sugar
- 100ml double cream

Instruction:

1. Rinse the fresh blueberries under cold water and drain them.
2. In a blender, combine the blueberries, whole milk, and caster sugar. Blend until smooth.
3. Pour the blueberry mixture into a saucepan and heat over low heat, stirring constantly, until the sugar is dissolved.
4. Remove the blueberry mixture from heat and allow it to cool to room temperature.
5. Once cooled, stir in the double cream until well combined.
6. Pour the blueberry mixture into the Ninja CREAMi tub.
7. Place the lid on the tub and freeze for at least 24 hours.
8. Remove the tub from the freezer and let it sit at room temperature for a few minutes. Remove the lid from the tub.
9. Select the "GELATO" program on your Ninja CREAMi.
10. Once processing is complete, serve the blueberry gelato immediately.

Per Serving

Calories: 180; Fat: 7g;
Carbohydrates: 27g; Protein: 2g

Pineapple Gelato

 Serves: 4 ; Prep: 15 Min

Ingredient

- 1 medium ripe pineapple
- 200ml whole milk
- 100g caster sugar
- 100ml double cream

 Instruction:

1. Peel and core the ripe pineapple, then cut it into small chunks.
2. In a blender, combine the pineapple chunks, whole milk, and caster sugar. Blend until smooth.
3. Pour the pineapple mixture into a saucepan and heat over low heat, stirring constantly, until the sugar is dissolved.
4. Remove the pineapple mixture from heat and allow it to cool to room temperature.
5. Once cooled, stir in the double cream until well combined.
6. Pour the pineapple mixture into the Ninja CREAMi tub.
7. Place the lid on the tub and freeze for at least 24 hours.
8. Remove the tub from the freezer and let it sit at room temperature for a few minutes. Remove the lid from the tub.
9. Select the "GELATO" program on your Ninja CREAMi.
10. Once processing is complete, serve the pineapple gelato immediately.

Per Serving

Calories: 150; Fat: 6g;
Carbohydrates: 24g; Protein: 2g

CHAPTER 04: GELATO

Watermelon Gelato

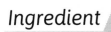 Serves: 4 ; Prep: 10 Min

Ingredient

- 500g watermelon flesh, seedless
- 100g caster sugar
- 200ml double cream
- 100ml whole milk

Instruction:

1. Cut the seedless watermelon flesh into chunks.
2. In a blender, combine the watermelon chunks and caster sugar. Blend until smooth.
3. Add the double cream and whole milk to the blender with the watermelon mixture. Blend until well combined.
4. Pour the mixture into the Ninja CREAMi tub.
5. Place the lid on the tub and freeze for at least 24 hours.
6. After freezing, remove the tub from the freezer and let it sit at room temperature for a few minutes.
7. Remove the lid from the tub and select the "GELATO" program on your Ninja CREAMi.
8. Once processing is complete, serve the watermelon gelato immediately.

Per Serving

Calories: 190; Fat: 10g;
Carbohydrates: 25g; Protein: 2g

Passion Fruit Gelato

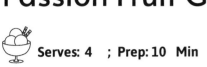

Serves: 4 ; Prep: 10 Min

Ingredient

- 200ml passion fruit juice (freshly squeezed or store-bought)
- 100g caster sugar
- 200ml double cream
- 100ml whole milk

Instruction:

1. In a mixing bowl, combine the passion fruit juice and caster sugar. Stir until the sugar is fully dissolved.
2. Add the double cream and whole milk to the bowl with the passion fruit mixture. Stir until well combined.
3. Pour the mixture into the Ninja CREAMi tub.
4. Place the lid on the tub and freeze for at least 24 hours.
5. After freezing, remove the tub from the freezer and let it sit at room temperature for a few minutes.
6. Remove the lid from the tub and select the "GELATO" program on your Ninja CREAMi.
7. Once processing is complete, serve the passion fruit gelato immediately.

Per Serving

Calories: 240; Fat: 14g;
Carbohydrates: 27g; Protein: 2g

CHAPTER 04: GELATO

Pomegranate Gelato

Serves: 4 ; Prep: 10 Min

Ingredient

- 300ml pomegranate juice
- 100g caster sugar
- 200ml double cream
- 100ml whole milk

Instruction:

1. In a mixing bowl, combine the pomegranate juice and caster sugar. Stir until the sugar is fully dissolved.
2. Add the double cream and whole milk to the bowl with the pomegranate mixture. Stir until well combined.
3. Pour the mixture into the Ninja CREAMi tub.
4. Place the lid on the tub and freeze for at least 24 hours.
5. After freezing, remove the tub from the freezer and let it sit at room temperature for a few minutes.
6. Remove the lid from the tub and select the "GELATO" program on your Ninja CREAMi.
7. Once processing is complete, serve the pomegranate gelato immediately.

Per Serving

Calories: 250; Fat: 14g;
Carbohydrates: 30g; Protein: 2g

Kiwi Gelato

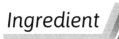 Serves: 4 ; Prep: 15 Min

Ingredient

- 4 ripe kiwis
- 100g caster sugar
- 200ml double cream
- 100ml whole milk

Instruction:

1. Peel the kiwis and cut them into small pieces.
2. In a blender, combine the kiwi pieces and caster sugar. Blend until smooth.
3. Add the double cream and whole milk to the blender with the kiwi mixture. Blend until well combined.
4. Pour the mixture into the Ninja CREAMi tub.
5. Place the lid on the tub and freeze for at least 24 hours.
6. After freezing, remove the tub from the freezer and let it sit at room temperature for a few minutes.
7. Remove the lid from the tub and select the "GELATO" program on your Ninja CREAMi.
8. Once processing is complete, serve the kiwi gelato immediately.

Per Serving

Calories: 220; Fat: 14g;
Carbohydrates: 22g; Protein: 2g

CHAPTER 04: GELATO

Peach Gelato

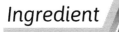 Serves: 4 ; Prep: 15 Min

Ingredient

- 4 ripe peaches
- 100g caster sugar
- 200ml double cream
- 100ml whole milk

Instruction:

1. Peel the peaches, remove the pits, and cut them into small pieces.
2. In a blender, combine the peach pieces and caster sugar. Blend until smooth.
3. Add the double cream and whole milk to the blender with the peach mixture. Blend until well combined.
4. Pour the mixture into the Ninja CREAMi tub.
5. Place the lid on the tub and freeze for at least 24 hours.
6. After freezing, remove the tub from the freezer and let it sit at room temperature for a few minutes.
7. Remove the lid from the tub and select the "GELATO" program on your Ninja CREAMi.
8. Once processing is complete, serve the peach gelato immediately.

Per Serving

Calories: 220; Fat: 14g;
Carbohydrates: 22g; Protein: 2g

Blackberry Gelato

Serves: 4 ; Prep: 15 Min

Ingredient

- 300g blackberries
- 100g caster sugar
- 200ml double cream
- 100ml whole milk

Per Serving

Calories: 180; Fat: 10g;
Carbohydrates: 21g; Protein: 2g

Instruction:

1. Rinse the blackberries under cold water and drain them.
2. In a blender, combine the blackberries and caster sugar. Blend until smooth.
3. Add the double cream and whole milk to the blender with the blackberry mixture. Blend until well combined.
4. Pour the mixture into the Ninja CREAMi tub.
5. Place the lid on the tub and freeze for at least 24 hours.
6. After freezing, remove the tub from the freezer and let it sit at room temperature for a few minutes.
7. Remove the lid from the tub and select the "GELATO" program on your Ninja CREAMi.
8. Once processing is complete, serve the blackberry gelato immediately.

CHAPTER 04: GELATO

Lime Gelato

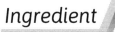

Serves: 4 ; Prep: 15 Min

Ingredient

- 3 large egg yolks
- 80g caster sugar
- 200ml double cream
- 170ml whole milk
- Zest and juice of 2 limes

Per Serving

Calories: 250; Fat: 18g;
Carbohydrates: 20g; Protein: 4g

Instruction:

1. In a small saucepan, whisk together the egg yolks and caster sugar until well combined.
2. Add the double cream, whole milk, lime zest, and lime juice to the saucepan. Stir to combine.
3. Place the saucepan on the hob over medium heat, stirring constantly with a whisk or silicone spatula. Cook until the temperature reaches 165-175°F (74-79°C) on an instant-read thermometer.
4. Remove the base from heat and pour it through a fine-mesh sieve into an empty tub. Place the tub into an ice bath to cool down.
5. Once cooled, place the lid on the tub and freeze for at least 24 hours.
6. After freezing, remove the tub from the freezer and let it sit at room temperature for a few minutes.
7. Remove the lid from the tub and select the "GELATO" program on your Ninja CREAMi.
8. Once processing is complete, serve the lime gelato immediately.

Classic Vanilla Milkshake

 Serves: 1 ; Prep: 05 Min

Ingredient

- 200ml vanilla ice cream
- 120ml whole milk

 **Instruction:**

1. Place 200ml vanilla ice cream and 120ml whole milk in the empty container.
2. Follow the quick instructions for assembly and processing.
3. Select the "MILKSHAKE" program.
4. Once processing is complete, add any mix-ins if desired.
5. Serve immediately.

Per Serving

Calories: 280; Fat: 15g;
Carbohydrates: 28g; Protein: 7g

CHAPTER 05: MILKSHAKE

Chocolate Milkshake

 Serves: 1 ; Prep: 05 Min

Ingredient

- 200ml chocolate ice cream
- 120ml whole milk

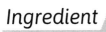 **Instruction:**

1. Place 200ml chocolate ice cream and 120ml whole milk in the empty container.
2. Follow the quick instructions for assembly and processing.
3. Select the "MILKSHAKE" program.
4. Once processing is complete, add any mix-ins if desired.
5. Serve immediately.

Per Serving

Calories: 380; Fat: 20g;
Carbohydrates: 35g; Protein: 9g

Strawberry Milkshake

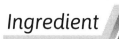 Serves: 1 ; Prep: 05 Min

Ingredient

 **Instruction:**

1. Add 200ml strawberry ice cream, 120ml whole milk, and 100g fresh strawberries to the empty container in the order listed.
2. Follow the quick instructions for assembly and processing.
3. Select the "MILKSHAKE" program.
4. Once processing is complete, add any mix-ins if desired.
5. Serve immediately.

- 200ml strawberry ice cream
- 120ml whole milk
- 100g fresh strawberries, stems removed and halved

Per Serving

Calories: 300; Fat: 14g;
Carbohydrates: 36g; Protein: 6g

CHAPTER 05: MILKSHAKE

Banana Milkshake

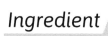 Serves: 1 ; Prep: 05 Min

Ingredient

Instruction:

1. Add 1 large banana (sliced), 200ml vanilla ice cream, and 120ml whole milk to the empty container in the order listed.
2. Follow the quick instructions for assembly and processing.
3. Select the "MILKSHAKE" program.
4. Once processing is complete, add any mix-ins if desired.
5. Serve immediately.

- 1 large banana, peeled and sliced
- 200ml vanilla ice cream
- 120ml whole milk

Per Serving

Calories: 330; Fat: 16g;
Carbohydrates: 44g; Protein: 6g

Peanut Butter Milkshake

 Serves: 1 ; Prep: 05 Min

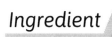 *Ingredient*

- 2 tablespoons (30g) peanut butter
- 200ml vanilla ice cream
- 120ml whole milk

 Instruction:

1. Add 2 tablespoons of peanut butter, 200ml vanilla ice cream, and 120ml whole milk to the empty container in the order listed.
2. Follow the quick instructions for assembly and processing.
3. Select the "MILKSHAKE" program.
4. Once processing is complete, add any mix-ins if desired.
5. Serve immediately.

Per Serving

Calories: 460; Fat: 31g;
Carbohydrates: 32g; Protein: 14g

CHAPTER 05: MILKSHAKE

Cookies and Cream Milkshake

 Serves: 1   ; Prep: 05 Min

 *Ingredient*

- 2 chocolate sandwich cookies (Oreo or similar)
- 200ml vanilla ice cream
- 120ml whole milk

Instruction:

1. Crush 2 chocolate sandwich cookies and add them to the empty container.
2. Add 200ml vanilla ice cream and 120ml whole milk to the container.
3. Follow the quick instructions for assembly and processing.
4. Select the "MILKSHAKE" program.
5. Once processing is complete, serve immediately.

Per Serving

Calories: 440; Fat: 25g;
Carbohydrates: 46g; Protein: 8g

Mint Chocolate Chip Milkshake

Instruction:

 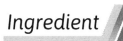

Serves: 1 ; Prep: 05 Min

Ingredient

- 1 tablespoon (15ml) mint extract
- 50g dark chocolate chips
- 200ml vanilla ice cream
- 120ml whole milk

1. Add 1 tablespoon of mint extract and 50g of dark chocolate chips to the empty container.
2. Add 200ml vanilla ice cream and 120ml whole milk to the container.
3. Follow the quick instructions for assembly and processing.
4. Select the "MILKSHAKE" program.
5. Once processing is complete, serve immediately.

Per Serving

Calories: 450; Fat: 26g;
Carbohydrates: 45g; Protein: 8g

CHAPTER 05: MILKSHAKE

Coffee Milkshake

Instruction:

 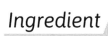

Serves: 1 ; Prep: 05 Min

Ingredient

- 120ml brewed coffee, chilled
- 200ml vanilla ice cream
- 120ml whole milk

1. Brew coffee and chill it.
2. Add 120ml of chilled brewed coffee, 200ml vanilla ice cream, and 120ml whole milk to the empty container in the order listed.
3. Follow the quick instructions for assembly and processing.
4. Select the "MILKSHAKE" program.
5. Once processing is complete, serve immediately.

Per Serving

Calories: 320; Fat: 17g;
Carbohydrates: 36g; Protein: 6g

Salted Caramel Milkshake

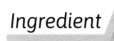 **Serves: 1 ; Prep: 05 Min**

Ingredient

- 2 tablespoons (30ml) salted caramel sauce
- 200ml vanilla ice cream
- 120ml whole milk

Instruction:

1. Add 2 tablespoons of salted caramel sauce, 200ml vanilla ice cream, and 120ml whole milk to the empty container in the order listed.
2. Follow the quick instructions for assembly and processing.
3. Select the "MILKSHAKE" program.
4. Once processing is complete, serve immediately.

Per Serving

Calories: 410; Fat: 20g;
Carbohydrates: 52g; Protein: 7g

CHAPTER 05: MILKSHAKE

Coconut Milkshake

Instruction:

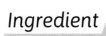 **Serves: 1 ; Prep: 05 Min**

Ingredient

- 120ml coconut milk
- 200ml vanilla ice cream
- 120ml whole milk

1. Add 120ml coconut milk, 200ml vanilla ice cream, and 120ml whole milk to the empty container in the order listed.
2. Follow the quick instructions for assembly and processing.
3. Select the "MILKSHAKE" program.
4. Once processing is complete, serve immediately.

Per Serving

Calories: 470; Fat: 31g;
Carbohydrates: 36g; Protein: 8g

Almond Milkshake

 **Serves: 1 ; Prep: 05 Min**

Ingredient

- 120ml almond milk
- 200ml vanilla ice cream
- 120ml whole milk

 Instruction:

1. Add 120ml almond milk, 200ml vanilla ice cream, and 120ml whole milk to the empty container in the order listed.
2. Follow the quick instructions for assembly and processing.
3. Select the "MILKSHAKE" program.
4. Once processing is complete, serve immediately.

Per Serving

Calories: 400; Fat: 25g;
Carbohydrates: 36g; Protein: 7g

CHAPTER 05: MILKSHAKE

Raspberry Milkshake

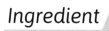 **Serves: 1 ; Prep: 05 Min**

Ingredient

- 100g fresh raspberries
- 200ml vanilla ice cream
- 120ml whole milk

Instruction:

1. Add 100g fresh raspberries, 200ml vanilla ice cream, and 120ml whole milk to the empty container in the order listed.
2. Follow the quick instructions for assembly and processing.
3. Select the "MILKSHAKE" program.
4. Once processing is complete, serve immediately.

Per Serving

Calories: 320; Fat: 16g;
Carbohydrates: 38g; Protein: 6g

Blueberry Milkshake

Serves: 1 ; Prep: 05 Min

Ingredient

- 100g fresh blueberries
- 200ml vanilla ice cream
- 120ml whole milk

 Instruction:

1. Add 100g fresh blueberries, 200ml vanilla ice cream, and 120ml whole milk to the empty container in the order listed.
2. Follow the quick instructions for assembly and processing.
3. Select the "MILKSHAKE" program.
4. Once processing is complete, serve immediately.

Per Serving

Calories: 330; Fat: 16g;
Carbohydrates: 38g; Protein: 6g

CHAPTER 05: MILKSHAKE

Pineapple Milkshake

Serves: 1 ; Prep: 05 Min

Ingredient

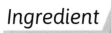

- 100g fresh pineapple chunks
- 200ml vanilla ice cream
- 120ml whole milk

Instruction:

1. Add 100g fresh pineapple chunks, 200ml vanilla ice cream, and 120ml whole milk to the empty container in the order listed.
2. Follow the quick instructions for assembly and processing.
3. Select the "MILKSHAKE" program.
4. Once processing is complete, serve immediately.

Per Serving

Calories: 330; Fat: 16g;
Carbohydrates: 40g; Protein: 6g

Mango Milkshake

 **Serves: 1 ; Prep: 05 Min**

Ingredient

- 100g fresh mango chunks
- 200ml vanilla ice cream
- 120ml whole milk

 **_Instruction:_**

1. Add 100g fresh mango chunks, 200ml vanilla ice cream, and 120ml whole milk to the empty container in the order listed.
2. Follow the quick instructions for assembly and processing.
3. Select the "MILKSHAKE" program.
4. Once processing is complete, serve immediately.

<u>Per Serving</u>

Calories: 340; Fat: 16g;
Carbohydrates: 42g; Protein: 6g

CHAPTER 05: MILKSHAKE

Peach Milkshake

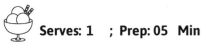 **Serves: 1 ; Prep: 05 Min**

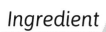
Ingredient

- 100g fresh peach slices
- 200ml vanilla ice cream
- 120ml whole milk

Instruction:

1. Add 100g fresh peach slices, 200ml vanilla ice cream, and 120ml whole milk to the empty container in the order listed.
2. Follow the quick instructions for assembly and processing.
3. Select the "MILKSHAKE" program.
4. Once processing is complete, serve immediately.

<u>Per Serving</u>

Calories: 330; Fat: 16g;
Carbohydrates: 40g; Protein: 6g

Blackberry Milkshake

 Serves: 1 ; Prep: 05 Min

Ingredient

- 100g fresh blackberries
- 200ml vanilla ice cream
- 120ml whole milk

Instruction:

1. Add 100g fresh blackberries, 200ml vanilla ice cream, and 120ml whole milk to the empty container in the order listed.
2. Follow the quick instructions for assembly and processing.
3. Select the "MILKSHAKE" program.
4. Once processing is complete, serve immediately.

Per Serving

Calories: 330; Fat: 16g;
Carbohydrates: 40g; Protein: 6g

CHAPTER 05: MILKSHAKE

Cherry Milkshake

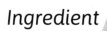 Serves: 1 ; Prep: 05 Min

Ingredient

- 100g fresh cherries, pitted
- 200ml vanilla ice cream
- 120ml whole milk

Instruction:

1. Add 100g fresh cherries, pitted, 200ml vanilla ice cream, and 120ml whole milk to the empty container in the order listed.
2. Follow the quick instructions for assembly and processing.
3. Select the "MILKSHAKE" program.
4. Once processing is complete, serve immediately.

Per Serving

Calories: 330; Fat: 16g;
Carbohydrates: 40g; Protein: 6g

Orange Creamsicle Milkshake

Serves: 1 ; Prep: 05 Min

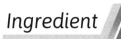

Ingredient

- 1 large orange, peeled and segmented
- 200ml vanilla ice cream
- 120ml whole milk

 Instruction:

1. Add 1 large orange, peeled and segmented, 200ml vanilla ice cream, and 120ml whole milk to the empty container in the order listed.
2. Follow the quick instructions for assembly and processing.
3. Select the "MILKSHAKE" program.
4. Once processing is complete, serve immediately.

Per Serving

Calories: 320; Fat: 16g;
Carbohydrates: 40g; Protein: 6g

CHAPTER 05: MILKSHAKE

Key Lime Pie Milkshake

Serves: 1 ; Prep: 05 Min

Ingredient

- 2 ripe key limes, juiced
- Zest of 1 key lime
- 200ml vanilla ice cream
- 120ml whole milk
- 2 tablespoons graham cracker crumbs
- Optional: whipped cream for topping

Instruction:

1. Juice 2 ripe key limes and zest one key lime.
2. Add the lime juice, lime zest, 200ml vanilla ice cream, 120ml whole milk, and 2 tablespoons graham cracker crumbs to the empty container in the order listed.
3. Follow the quick instructions for assembly and processing.
4. Select the "MILKSHAKE" program.
5. Once processing is complete, serve immediately. Optionally, top with whipped cream and additional graham cracker crumbs.

Per Serving

Calories: 340; Fat: 16g;
Carbohydrates: 42g; Protein: 6g

Acai Berry Smoothie Bowl

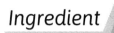 Serves: 2 ; Prep: 05 Min

Ingredient

- 100g frozen acai berries
- 1 ripe banana, sliced
- 50g blueberries
- 100ml coconut milk
- Toppings (optional): Sliced banana, Fresh berries, Granola

Per Serving

Calories: 150; Fat: 7g;
Carbohydrates: 20g; Protein: 2g

 ## Instruction:

1. Fill an empty container with frozen acai berries, sliced banana, and blueberries.
2. Pour coconut milk over the fruit until covered. Place the lid on the tub and freeze for 24 hours.
3. Remove the tub from the freezer and remove the lid. Follow the quick instructions for assembly and processing.
4. Select the SMOOTHIE BOWL program.
5. Once processing is complete, transfer the smoothie base to a bowl and garnish with sliced banana, fresh berries, and granola.

CHAPTER 06: SMOOTHIE BOWL

Peanut Butter Banana Smoothie Bowl

 Serves: 2 ; Prep: 05 Min

Ingredient

- 2 ripe bananas, sliced
- 30g peanut butter
- 150ml almond milk
- 1 tbsp honey (optional)
- Toppings (optional): Sliced banana, Peanut butter drizzle, Granola

Per Serving

Calories: 250; Fat: 12g;
Carbohydrates: 30g; Protein: 5g

 ## Instruction:

1. Fill an empty container with sliced bananas.
2. Add peanut butter and almond milk. Optionally, add honey for sweetness.
3. Place the lid on the tub and freeze for 24 hours.
4. Remove the tub from the freezer and remove the lid. Follow the quick instructions for assembly and processing.
5. Select the SMOOTHIE BOWL program.
6. Once processing is complete, transfer the smoothie base to a bowl and garnish with sliced banana, a drizzle of peanut butter, and granola.

Strawberry Banana Smoothie Bowl

Serves: 2 ; Prep: 05 Min

Ingredient

- 120g strawberries, sliced
- 1 ripe banana, sliced
- 150ml yogurt
- 100ml whole milk
- Toppings (optional): Sliced banana, Strawberry slices, Roasted flaked almonds

<u>Per Serving</u>

Calories: 150; Fat: 4g;
Carbohydrates: 22g; Protein: 6g

 ## Instruction:

1. Fill an empty container with sliced strawberries and bananas.
2. Pour yogurt and milk over the fruit. Place the lid on the tub and freeze for 24 hours.
3. Remove the tub from the freezer and remove the lid. Follow the quick instructions for assembly and processing.
4. Select the SMOOTHIE BOWL program.
5. Once processing is complete, transfer the smoothie base to a bowl and garnish with sliced banana, strawberry slices, and roasted flaked almonds.

CHAPTER 06: SMOOTHIE BOWL

Blueberry Almond Smoothie Bowl

Serves: 2 ; Prep: 05 Min

Ingredient

- 120g blueberries
- 30g almond butter
- 150ml almond milk
- 1 tbsp honey (optional)
- Toppings (optional): Sliced almonds, Fresh blueberries, Honey drizzle

<u>Per Serving</u>

Calories: 200; Fat: 10g;
Carbohydrates: 25g; Protein: 5g

Instruction:

1. Fill an empty container with blueberries.
2. Add almond butter and almond milk. Optionally, add honey for sweetness.
3. Place the lid on the tub and freeze for 24 hours.
4. Remove the tub from the freezer and remove the lid. Follow the quick instructions for assembly and processing.
5. Select the SMOOTHIE BOWL program.
6. Once processing is complete, transfer the smoothie base to a bowl and garnish with sliced almonds, fresh blueberries, and a drizzle of honey.

Mango Coconut Smoothie Bowl

Serves: 2   ; Prep: 05 Min

Ingredient

- 150g mango chunks
- 50g shredded coconut
- 150ml coconut milk
- 100ml coconut water
- Toppings (optional): Sliced mango, Toasted coconut flakes, Chia seeds

Per Serving

Calories: 250; Fat: 15g;
Carbohydrates: 30g; Protein: 3g

 Instruction:

1. Fill an empty container with mango chunks and shredded coconut.
2. Pour coconut milk and coconut water over the fruit and coconut. Place the lid on the tub and freeze for 24 hours.
3. Remove the tub from the freezer and remove the lid. Follow the quick instructions for assembly and processing.
4. Select the SMOOTHIE BOWL program.
5. Once processing is complete, transfer the smoothie base to a bowl and garnish with sliced mango, toasted coconut flakes, and chia seeds.

CHAPTER 06: SMOOTHIE BOWL

Peach Raspberry Smoothie Bowl

Serves: 2   ; Prep: 05 Min

Ingredient

- 150g ripe peaches, sliced
- 100g raspberries
- 150ml Greek yogurt
- 100ml almond milk
- Toppings (optional): Sliced peaches, Fresh raspberries, Granola

Per Serving

Calories: 180; Fat: 5g;
Carbohydrates: 25g; Protein: 10g

Instruction:

1. Fill an empty container with sliced peaches and raspberries.
2. Add Greek yogurt and almond milk over the fruit. Place the lid on the tub and freeze for 24 hours.
3. Remove the tub from the freezer and remove the lid. Follow the quick instructions for assembly and processing.
4. Select the SMOOTHIE BOWL program.
5. Once processing is complete, transfer the smoothie base to a bowl and garnish with sliced peaches, fresh raspberries, and granola.

Mixed Berry Smoothie Bowl

  Serves: 2 ; Prep: 05 Min

Ingredient

- 100g strawberries, sliced
- 50g raspberries
- 50g blueberries
- 150ml Greek yogurt
- 100ml almond milk
- Toppings (optional): Sliced strawberries, Fresh raspberries, Fresh blueberries, Granola

Per Serving

Calories: 180; Fat: 5g;
Carbohydrates: 25g; Protein: 10g

 **Instruction:**

1. Fill an empty container with sliced strawberries, raspberries, and blueberries.
2. Add Greek yogurt and almond milk over the fruit. Place the lid on the tub and freeze for 24 hours.
3. Remove the tub from the freezer and remove the lid. Follow the quick instructions for assembly and processing.
4. Select the SMOOTHIE BOWL program.
5. Once processing is complete, transfer the smoothie base to a bowl and garnish with sliced strawberries, fresh raspberries, fresh blueberries, and granola.

CHAPTER 06: SMOOTHIE BOWL

Chocolate Peanut Butter Smoothie Bowl

  Serves: 2 ; Prep: 05 Min

Ingredient

- 30g peanut butter
- 15g cocoa powder
- 150ml almond milk
- 1 ripe banana, sliced
- Toppings (optional): Sliced banana, Peanut butter drizzle, Dark chocolate shavings

 Instruction:

1. Fill an empty container with peanut butter, cocoa powder, almond milk, and sliced banana.
2. Place the lid on the tub and freeze for 24 hours.
3. Remove the tub from the freezer and remove the lid. Follow the quick instructions for assembly and processing.
4. Select the SMOOTHIE BOWL program.
5. Once processing is complete, transfer the smoothie base to a bowl and garnish with sliced banana, a drizzle of peanut butter, and dark chocolate shavings.

Per Serving

Calories: 200; Fat: 10g;
Carbohydrates: 25g; Protein: 5g

Pineapple Coconut Smoothie Bowl

Serves: 2 ; Prep: 05 Min

Ingredient

- 150g pineapple chunks
- 50g shredded coconut
- 150ml coconut milk
- 100ml coconut water
- Toppings (optional): Sliced pineapple, Toasted coconut flakes, Chia seeds

Per Serving

Calories: 250; Fat: 15g;
Carbohydrates: 30g; Protein: 3g

 ## Instruction:

1. Fill an empty container with pineapple chunks and shredded coconut.
2. Pour coconut milk and coconut water over the fruit and coconut. Place the lid on the tub and freeze for 24 hours.
3. Remove the tub from the freezer and remove the lid. Follow the quick instructions for assembly and processing.
4. Select the SMOOTHIE BOWL program.
5. Once processing is complete, transfer the smoothie base to a bowl and garnish with sliced pineapple, toasted coconut flakes, and chia seeds.

CHAPTER 06: SMOOTHIE BOWL

Matcha Green Tea Smoothie Bowl

Serves: 2 ; Prep: 05 Min

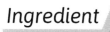

Ingredient

- 2 tsp matcha green tea powder
- 1 ripe banana, sliced
- 150ml almond milk
- 100ml Greek yogurt
- Toppings (optional): Sliced banana, Granola, Chia seeds

Per Serving

Calories: 150; Fat: 5g;
Carbohydrates: 20g; Protein: 5g

Instruction:

1. Fill an empty container with matcha green tea powder and sliced banana.
2. Pour almond milk and Greek yogurt over the ingredients. Place the lid on the tub and freeze for 24 hours.
3. Remove the tub from the freezer and remove the lid. Follow the quick instructions for assembly and processing.
4. Select the SMOOTHIE BOWL program.
5. Once processing is complete, transfer the smoothie base to a bowl and garnish with sliced banana, granola, and chia seeds.

Strawberry Kiwi Smoothie Bowl

Serves: 2 ; Prep: 05 Min

Ingredient

- 100g strawberries, sliced
- 2 kiwis, peeled and sliced
- 150ml Greek yogurt
- 100ml almond milk
- Toppings (optional): Sliced strawberries, Sliced kiwi, Granola

Per Serving

Calories: 120; Fat: 3g;
Carbohydrates: 18g; Protein: 7g

 Instruction:

1. Fill an empty container with sliced strawberries and kiwis.
2. Pour Greek yogurt and almond milk over the fruit. Place the lid on the tub and freeze for 24 hours.
3. Remove the tub from the freezer and remove the lid. Follow the quick instructions for assembly and processing.
4. Select the SMOOTHIE BOWL program.
5. Once processing is complete, transfer the smoothie base to a bowl and garnish with sliced strawberries, sliced kiwi, and granola.

CHAPTER 06: SMOOTHIE BOWL

Peach Mango Smoothie Bowl

Serves: 2 ; Prep: 05 Min

Ingredient

- 150g ripe mango, diced
- 150g ripe peaches, diced
- 150ml Greek yogurt
- 100ml almond milk
- Toppings (optional): Sliced mango, Sliced peaches, Granola

Per Serving

Calories: 150; Fat: 3g;
Carbohydrates: 25g; Protein: 7g

Instruction:

1. Fill an empty container with diced mango and peaches.
2. Pour Greek yogurt and almond milk over the fruit. Place the lid on the tub and freeze for 24 hours.
3. Remove the tub from the freezer and remove the lid. Follow the quick instructions for assembly and processing.
4. Select the SMOOTHIE BOWL program.
5. Once processing is complete, transfer the smoothie base to a bowl and garnish with sliced mango, sliced peaches, and granola.

Cherry Almond Smoothie Bowl

  Serves: 2 ; Prep: 05 Min

Ingredient

- 150g cherries, pitted
- 30g almond butter
- 150ml almond milk
- 100ml Greek yogurt
- Toppings (optional): Sliced cherries, Almond slices, Honey drizzle

<u>Per Serving</u>

Calories: 200; Fat: 10g;
Carbohydrates: 25g; Protein: 7g

 ## Instruction:

1. Fill an empty container with pitted cherries and almond butter.
2. Pour almond milk and Greek yogurt over the cherries and almond butter. Place the lid on the tub and freeze for 24 hours.
3. Remove the tub from the freezer and remove the lid. Follow the quick instructions for assembly and processing.
4. Select the SMOOTHIE BOWL program.
5. Once processing is complete, transfer the smoothie base to a bowl and garnish with sliced cherries, almond slices, and a drizzle of honey.

CHAPTER 06: SMOOTHIE BOWL

Raspberry Coconut Smoothie Bowl

  Serves: 2 ; Prep: 05 Min

Ingredient

- 150g raspberries
- 30g shredded coconut
- 150ml coconut milk
- 100ml Greek yogurt
- Toppings (optional): Fresh raspberries, Toasted coconut flakes, Chia seeds

<u>Per Serving</u>

Calories: 180; Fat: 10g;
Carbohydrates: 15g; Protein: 5g

 ## Instruction:

1. Fill an empty container with raspberries and shredded coconut.
2. Pour coconut milk and Greek yogurt over the raspberries and coconut. Place the lid on the tub and freeze for 24 hours.
3. Remove the tub from the freezer and remove the lid. Follow the quick instructions for assembly and processing.
4. Select the SMOOTHIE BOWL program.
5. Once processing is complete, transfer the smoothie base to a bowl and garnish with fresh raspberries, toasted coconut flakes, and chia seeds.

Banana Berry Smoothie Bowl

Serves: 2 ; **Prep: 05 Min**

Ingredient

- 1 ripe banana, sliced
- 100g mixed berries
  (such as strawberries, raspberries, blueberries)
- 150ml Greek yogurt
- 100ml almond milk
- Toppings (optional): Sliced banana, Mixed berries, Granola

Per Serving

Calories: 150; Fat: 4g;
Carbohydrates: 25g; Protein: 8g

Instruction:

1. Fill an empty container with sliced banana and mixed berries.
2. Pour Greek yogurt and almond milk over the fruit. Place the lid on the tub and freeze for 24 hours.
3. Remove the tub from the freezer and remove the lid. Follow the quick instructions for assembly and processing.
4. Select the SMOOTHIE BOWL program.
5. Once processing is complete, transfer the smoothie base to a bowl and garnish with sliced banana, mixed berries, and granola.

CHAPTER 06: SMOOTHIE BOWL

Pineapple Spinach Smoothie Bowl

Serves: 2 ; **Prep: 05 Min**

Ingredient

- 150g pineapple chunks
- 50g fresh spinach leaves
- 150ml coconut milk
- 100ml Greek yogurt
- Toppings (optional): Sliced pineapple, Fresh berries, Coconut flakes

Per Serving

Calories: 150; Fat: 6g;
Carbohydrates: 20g; Protein: 5g

Instruction:

1. Fill an empty container with pineapple chunks and fresh spinach leaves.
2. Pour coconut milk and Greek yogurt over the pineapple and spinach. Place the lid on the tub and freeze for 24 hours.
3. Remove the tub from the freezer and remove the lid. Follow the quick instructions for assembly and processing.
4. Select the SMOOTHIE BOWL program.
5. Once processing is complete, transfer the smoothie base to a bowl and garnish with sliced pineapple, fresh berries, and coconut flakes.

Blueberry Avocado Smoothie Bowl

 **Serves: 2 ; Prep: 05 Min**

Ingredient

- 150g blueberries
- 1 ripe avocado, peeled and pitted
- 150ml almond milk
- 100ml Greek yogurt
- Toppings (optional): Sliced banana, Granola, Chia seeds

Per Serving

Calories: 180; Fat: 12g;
Carbohydrates: 15g; Protein: 6g

 ## Instruction:

1. Fill an empty container with blueberries and chopped avocado.
2. Pour almond milk and Greek yogurt over the blueberries and avocado. Place the lid on the tub and freeze for 24 hours.
3. Remove the tub from the freezer and remove the lid. Follow the quick instructions for assembly and processing.
4. Select the SMOOTHIE BOWL program.
5. Once processing is complete, transfer the smoothie base to a bowl and garnish with sliced banana, granola, and chia seeds.

CHAPTER 06: SMOOTHIE BOWL

Apple Cinnamon Smoothie Bowl

 **Serves: 2 ; Prep: 05 Min**

Ingredient

- 2 medium apples, peeled, cored, and chopped
- 1 teaspoon ground cinnamon
- 150ml almond milk
- 100g Greek yogurt
- Toppings (optional): Sliced almonds, Granola, Honey

Per Serving

Calories: 140; Fat: 4g;
Carbohydrates: 26g; Protein: 5g

Instruction:

1. Fill an empty container with chopped apples.
2. Sprinkle ground cinnamon over the apples.
3. Pour almond milk and Greek yogurt over the apples. Place the lid on the tub and freeze for 24 hours.
4. Remove the tub from the freezer and remove the lid. Follow the quick instructions for assembly and processing.
5. Select the SMOOTHIE BOWL program.
6. Once processing is complete, transfer the smoothie base to a bowl and garnish with sliced almonds, granola, and a drizzle of honey.

Orange Carrot Smoothie Bowl

 **Serves: 2 ; Prep: 05 Min**

Ingredient

- 2 medium carrots, peeled and chopped
- 2 oranges, peeled and segmented
- 150 ml coconut water
- 100 ml Greek yogurt
- Toppings (optional): Shredded coconut, Chia seeds, Orange slices

Per Serving

Calories: 120; Fat: 2g;
Carbohydrates: 24g; Protein: 4g

 ## Instruction:

1. Fill an empty container with chopped carrots and orange segments.
2. Pour coconut water and Greek yogurt over the carrots and oranges. Place the lid on the tub and freeze for 24 hours.
3. Remove the tub from the freezer and remove the lid. Follow the quick instructions for assembly and processing.
4. Select the SMOOTHIE BOWL program.
5. Once processing is complete, transfer the smoothie base to a bowl and garnish with shredded coconut, chia seeds, and orange slices.

CHAPTER 06: SMOOTHIE BOWL

Mixed Berry Spinach Smoothie Bowl

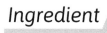 **Serves: 2 ; Prep: 05 Min**

Ingredient

- 150g mixed berries (such as strawberries, raspberries, and blueberries)
- 1 ripe banana, sliced
- 50g fresh spinach leaves
- 150 ml Greek yogurt
- 100 ml almond milk
- Toppings (optional): Granola, Sliced strawberries, Chia seeds

 ## Instruction:

1. Fill an empty container with mixed berries, sliced banana, and fresh spinach leaves.
2. Pour Greek yogurt and almond milk over the fruits and spinach. Place the lid on the tub and freeze for 24 hours.
3. Remove the tub from the freezer and remove the lid. Follow the quick instructions for assembly and processing.
4. Select the SMOOTHIE BOWL program.
5. Once processing is complete, transfer the smoothie base to a bowl and top with granola, sliced strawberries, and chia seeds.

Per Serving

Calories: 150; Fat: 2g;
Carbohydrates: 25g; Protein: 7g

Tropical Green Smoothie Bowl

Serves: 2 ; Prep: 05 Min

Ingredient

- 1 ripe banana, sliced
- 100g fresh pineapple chunks
- 50g mango chunks
- 50g fresh spinach leaves
- 150 ml coconut milk
- 100 ml pineapple juice
- Toppings (optional): Sliced kiwi, Shredded coconut, Chia seeds

 Instruction:

1. Fill an empty container with sliced banana, pineapple chunks, mango chunks, and fresh spinach leaves.
2. Pour coconut milk and pineapple juice over the fruits and spinach. Place the lid on the tub and freeze for 24 hours.
3. Remove the tub from the freezer and remove the lid. Follow the quick instructions for assembly and processing.
4. Select the SMOOTHIE BOWL program.
5. Once processing is complete, transfer the smoothie base to a bowl and top with sliced kiwi, shredded coconut, and chia seeds.

<u>Per Serving</u>

Calories: 180; Fat: 6g;
Carbohydrates: 30g; Protein: 3g

CHAPTER 06: SMOOTHIE BOWL

Kiwi Berry Smoothie Bowl

Serves: 2 ; Prep: 05 Min

Ingredient

- 2 ripe kiwis, peeled and sliced
- 100g mixed berries (such as strawberries, raspberries, and blueberries)
- 150 ml natural yogurt
- 100 ml almond milk
- 1 tablespoon honey (optional)
- Toppings (optional): Sliced kiwi, Mixed berries, Granola

Instruction:

1. Fill an empty container with sliced kiwis and mixed berries.
2. Pour natural yogurt and almond milk over the fruits. Add honey if desired. Place the lid on the tub and freeze for 24 hours.
3. Remove the tub from the freezer and remove the lid. Follow the quick instructions for assembly and processing.
4. Select the SMOOTHIE BOWL program.
5. Once processing is complete, transfer the smoothie base to a bowl and top with sliced kiwi, mixed berries, and granola.

<u>Per Serving</u>

Calories: 120; Fat: 2g;
Carbohydrates: 22g; Protein: 4g

Chocolate Cherry Smoothie Bowl

Serves: 2 ; Prep: 05 Min

Ingredient

- 100g pitted cherries
- 30g dark chocolate, chopped
- 150ml Greek yogurt
- 100ml almond milk
- Toppings (optional): Dark chocolate shavings, Fresh cherries, pitted and halved, Almond slices

<u>Per Serving</u>

Calories: 180; Fat: 8g;
Carbohydrates: 20g; Protein: 7g

Instruction:

1. Place pitted cherries and chopped dark chocolate into an empty container.
2. Pour Greek yogurt and almond milk over the cherries and chocolate.
3. Place the lid on the tub and freeze for 24 hours.
4. Remove the tub from the freezer and remove the lid.
5. Attach the creamerizer paddle and lid, then place it in your Ninja CREAMi.
6. Select the SMOOTHIE BOWL program.
7. Once processing is complete, spoon the processed base into a bowl.
8. Decorate with dark chocolate shavings, fresh cherries, and almond slices, if desired.

CHAPTER 06: SMOOTHIE BOWL

Pina Colada Smoothie Bowl

Serves: 2 ; Prep: 05 Min

Ingredient

- 100g fresh pineapple chunks
- 50g ripe banana, sliced
- 50ml coconut milk
- 50ml pineapple juice
- Toppings (optional): Toasted coconut flakes, Fresh pineapple chunks, Chopped macadamia nuts

<u>Per Serving</u>

Calories: 150; Fat: 7g;
Carbohydrates: 20g; Protein: 2g

Instruction:

1. Place fresh pineapple chunks and sliced banana into an empty container.
2. Pour coconut milk and pineapple juice over the fruits.
3. Place the lid on the tub and freeze for 24 hours.
4. Remove the tub from the freezer and remove the lid.
5. Attach the creamerizer paddle and lid, then place it in your Ninja CREAMi.
6. Select the SMOOTHIE BOWL program.
7. Once processing is complete, spoon the processed base into a bowl.
8. Decorate with toasted coconut flakes, fresh pineapple chunks, and chopped macadamia nuts, if desired.

Mix-in

Mix in chocolate, nuts, sweets, fruit and more to elevate any treat with bursts of flavour

Hard mix-ins
will remain intact.

Mix-ins like chocolate, sweets and nuts will not be broken down during the MIX-IN program. We recommend using mini chocolate chips, mini sweets or pre-chopped ingredients.

Soft mix-ins
will get broken down.

Mix-ins like cookies and frozen fruit will end up smaller after the MIX-IN program. We recommend using bigger pieces of soft ingredients

FOR ICE CREAM & GELATO ONLY

We don't recommend

fresh fruit, sauces and spreads to use as mix-ins.
Adding fresh fruit, fudge and caramel sauces will soften your treat. Chocolate hazelnut spread and nut butters generally do not incorporate well. We recommend using frozen fruit or chocolate/caramel shell toppings with the mix-in program and only enjoying sauces and spreads as toppings

Make one-of-a-kind treats
with extracts & mix-ins

1.
Make a base

Start by making any base from this guide & add an extract if desired.

To make even more flavours, substitute vanilla extract with 1 teaspoon of fruit, herb or nut extract.

2.
Freeze

Cover with lid and freeze for 24 hours

ICE CREAM	GELATO	LIGHT ICE CREAM

3.
Process

Select the program that matches your base
ICE CREAM
GELATO
LIGHT ICE CREAM

4.
Add mix-ins

With a spoon, create a 4cm wide hole that reaches the bottom of the tub.
Add your mix-ins to the hole in the tub.

+
MIX IN

5.
Process

Press MIX-IN program.

Don't want to wait? Scoop in some shop-bought ice cream into the tub and skip to step 4.

Creative with mix-ins

Mint Chocolate Chip	Strawberry	Chocolate Caramel Nut Cluster
Base: Vanilla (leave out vanilla extract) **Extract:** 1 tsp peppermint extract (Add green food colouring, optional) **Mix-in:** 45g mini chocolate chips	**Base:** Strawberry **Extract:** N/A **Mix-in:** 2 tbsp freeze dried strawberries or strawberry flakes	**Base:** Vanilla **Extract:** N/A **Mix-in:** 45g chocolate covered caramel sweets (broken), 2 tablespoons roasted hazelnuts (broken)
Sundae Cone	**Death by Chocolate**	**Banana Chocolate Chunk**
Base: Vanilla **Extract:** N/A **Mix-in:** 1 tbsp chocolate shell topping, 2 tbsp peanuts, 2 tbsp sugar cone pieces	**Base:** Chocolate **Extract:** N/A **Mix-in:** 2 tbsp mini chocolate chips, 2 tbsp brownie bits	**Base:** Vanilla, Chocolate **Extract:** N/A **Mix-in:** 1 tbsp banana chips, broken into pieces, 2 tbsp chocolate chips
Chocolate Chip Cookie Dough	**Chocolate Cookies & Cream**	**Orange Cream**
Base: Vanilla **Extract:** N/A **Mix-in:** 45g edible frozen cookie dough chunks + 1 tbsp mini chocolate chips	**Base:** Chocolate **Extract:** N/A **Mix-in:** 3 chocolate sandwich biscuits, broken	**Base:** Vanilla (leave out vanilla extract) **Extract:** 1 tsp orange extract **Mix-in:** N/A
Rum Raisin	**Lemon Vanilla**	**Salted Caramel**
Base: Vanilla **Extract:** N/A **Mix-in:** 40g raisins (soaked in 1 tsp rum)	**Base:** Vanilla (leave out vanilla extract) **Extract:** 1 tsp lemon extract **Mix-in:** N/A	**Base:** Chocolate **Extract:** N/A **Mix-in:** 2 tbsp salted caramel

Made in United States
Troutdale, OR
02/19/2025

29123920R00051